The Planet of the Apes

Jose Escobar

FADE IN

EXT. CONSTELLATION OF ORION - NIGHT
Stars glitter like diamonds on the black velvet backdrop of space.
The Belt of Orion is center screen, but much nearer and larger than ever seen by an Earth-bound astronomer.
A speck of light appears in the lower left corner of the screen.
No spaceship can be seen, but only a glowworm, a solitary sperma- tosoan gliding through the womb of the universe. Over this we HEAR the voice of an astronaut. He is concluding a report.

ASTRONAUT'S VOICE
(o. s.)
So ends my last signal until we reach our destination. We are now on automatic, a mere hundred and five light years from our base ... and at the mercy of com- puters. I've tucked in my crew for the long sleep. I'll join them presently.

INT. CABIN OF SPACESHIP - ESTABLISHING SHOT - NIGHT
The cabin is neither cramped nor spacious, but about the size of the President's cabin in Air Force One. In the immediate f. g. is a console of dials and switches flanked by four chairs. Only one of the chairs is occupied. The astronaut's back is to CAMERA. There is a ladder amidships which leads to an escape hatch. The after Dart of the cabin is obscured in darkness. We hear the MUSIC of a Mozart sonata emanating from a phonograph of stereotape. The astronaut is speaking into a microphone.

ASTRONAUT
Within the hour we shall complete the sixth month of our flight from
Cape Kennedy. By our time, that is ...
He pauses, looking up at:

TWO LARGE CLOCKS - ON CABIN WALL
One clock is marked SELF TIME, but instead of twelve numerals it has twenty-four.
One of the needles is moving very slowly.
The other clock is labeled EARTH TIME, and its units, like those of a
tachometer, are given by hundreds and thousands.
The largest needle of this clock makes one revolution every second.
Over this we hear:

ASTRONAUT'S VOICE
(o. s.)
But according to Dr. Hasslein theory of time in a vehicle traveling at close to the speed of light, old Mother Earth has aged a few thousand years since our de- parture -- while we have scarcely aged at all.

CLOSE ON ASTRONAUT
This is TAYLOR. He wears simple dungarees (or Churchill suit) and comfortable boots. He seems calm and pensive. Extracting the butt of a cigar from the breast pocket of his dungarees, he lights it, then continues:

TAYLOR
It may be so. This much is probable: the men who sent us on this journey have long since been moldering in forgotten graves; and those, if any, who read this message are a different breed. Hopefully, a better one.
He begins to roll up his left sleeve.

TAYLOR
I leave the twentieth century without regret. Who was it? Marshall? ... said
'Modern man is the missin 'a link between the ape and the human being. '
He removes the cigar from his mouth, turns to look out through one of the portholes into the astral night.

TAYLOR
One final thought -- nothing scientific, purely personal. Seen from up here, everything looks different ... Time bends and space is boundless. It squashes a man's ego. He begins to feel like no more than a mote in the eye of eternity. And he is nagged by a question: ahat if any- thing, will greet us on the end of man's first journey to a star? Are we to believe that throughout these thousands of galaxies, these millions of stars, only one, that speck of solar dust we call Earth, has been graced -- or cursed -- by human life?
(pause)
I have to doubt it.
He extracts a hypodermic needle from his breast pocket and injects it into the vein of his forearm. He continues speaking.

TAYLOR
(sardonically)
That's about all. I wonder if Man, that marvel of the universe, that glorious paradox who has sent me to the unknown... still makes war against his brother. , and lets his neighbor's children starve.
Taylor withdraws the hypodermic needle from his vein and secures it in a drawer of the console.

TAYLOR
Well then, Earthmen: A missing link salutes you. Bless you, my descendants.
Taylor snuffs out the cigar butt and places it in the drawer beside the

hypodermic. Then, flicking a switch Au cut off the Mozart, he rises and looks up again at:

THE CLOCK MARKED EARTH TIME
The longest needle of this clock now makes nearly two revolutions per second. The shortest needle points to the numeral .

INT. CABIN - TRACKING WITH TAYLOR
Space scientists have presumably solved the problem of weightlessness, for Taylor walks the short distance from; the console to the after section without particular effort. CAMERA FOLLOWS him, and we can now see four glass capsules, or "caskets", in the rear of the cabin. Taylor looks down at them.

-SEVERAL SHOTS - THE FOUR CASKETS - FROM TAYLOR'S P. O. V.
One of them is open. The other three are occupied by astronauts: DODGE,
LANDON and STEWART. They, too, wear dungarees and boots. Dodge and
Landon are thirtyish, clean-shaven, virile -- America's finest. Stewart is a handsome young woman, her hair bobbed short. Their eyes are closed and they do not appear to be breathing -- yet no undertaker could make them so alive.

ANOTHER ANGLE - FAVORING TAYLOR
He grasps the handle of his own casket and slowly pulls himself into
it. Continuing SILENCE. CAMERA MOVES IN as Taylor Dulls the glass lid
shut and secures it. He adjusts two dials inside the capsule and lies
back, buckling his safety belt. CAMERA MOVES INTO A CLOSEUP of Taylor.
His eyes are open. He seems serene, even enraptured.
(NOTE: Credits will appear here over a series of shots designed to
convey a sense of loneliness, of separation, and of the passage of
time.)

DISSOLVE TO:
-A SERIES OF SHOTS - A DISTANT GLOBE (MINIATURE)
We see a strange and distant planet. At first the globe occupies but a small area of the screen; but with each new VIEW it comes closer and
looms larger, as if' observed from a spaceship in a spiraling orbit of
descent.
The topography of the planet bears little resemblance to our own. Much
of it is obscured by cloud cover; even more of-it appears to be
cratered desert of reddish hue. We can, however, make out a few narrow
"green belts" and a patch of blue water.
In the FINAL SHOTS of this SEQUENCE we see the strange planet as it
would be observed from a spacecraft plummeting from twenty thousand

feet to one thousand feet. It appears that the ship will fall into a vast lake surrounded by soaring sandstone pinnacles. The water is blue-black, the pinnacles vermillion. (This is the Lake Powell
location, at Lone Rock.)

INT. SPACESHIP - FULL SHOT - DAY
Four empty pilot seats are seen in f. g. , the four glass caskets in b. g. We HEAR the RHYTHMIC BLEAT of a WARNING SIGNAL, a RUSH OF WIND as in a rapid descent, and perhaps the ROAR OF RETROJETS. Then, a great CRASH as the craft hits water. The whole ship shudders on impact.
Loose equipment falls to the cabin floor. CAMERA MOVES DOWN the cabin
aisle as the ship begins to roll in the water and HOLDS on the four glass caskets. There are THREE LOUD METALLIC CLICKS as the glass domes of the caskets swing open automatically.

CLOSE ON TAYLOR
He now has a full beard. His eyes come open. Instantly alert, he rises to a sitting position, gazing across at:

DODGE AND LANDON - FROM TAYLOR'S P. O. V.
They, too, awaken and sit up, starring at Taylor. They, too, are bearded.

TAYLOR'S VOICE
(o. s.)
You all right?
They nod.

BACK TO TAYLOR - CLOSE SHOT
He glances at the casket beside his own.

TAYLOR
Stewart?
(struggling to his feet)
Stewart?

CLOSE-SHOT --THE FOURTH CASKET
Its dome remains unopened. The young woman is a skeleton in a
Churchill suit.

REACTION SHOT - THE THREE ASTRONAUTS
Dodge and Landon have joined Taylor and-stare at the grinning skull of their dead comrade. A low, descending HUM of equipment is heard.
Simultaneously the lights begin to FADE. A moment later they brighten,

but not as much as before.

TAYLOR
There goes our primary power. We're on auxilliary.
A slight CRACKING sound is heard. Taylor turns quickly away and o. s. :

REVERSE ANGLE - THE FORWARD CABIN
A trickle of water has begun to seep through a ruptured seam in the
cabin. Taylor darts to a porthole and peers cut.

LONG SHOT - WHAT TAYLOR SEES:
water
The porthole is no more than six inches above the line. In the distance we discern a
shoreline of red desert.

TAYLOR'S VOICE
(o. s.)
We're in the soup. We're sinking.

INT. CABIN - FULL SHOT
The leak in the seam becomes a growing spray of water. Taylor turns away from the
porthole, calling:

TAYLOR
Dodge! Read the atmosphere!
Dodge moves instantly to the ladder beneath an escape hatch and mounts it. Taylor
stumbles down the aisle of the rolling ship toward
the console and addresses Landon, who is still staring at Stewart's skeleton.

TAYLOR
Landon! Send a last signal.

LANDON
(dazed)
What signal?

TAYLOR
To Earth! That we've landed!
As Landon lurches toward the communications equipment in f. g.

CUT TO:
**EXT. TIM STRANGE PLANET - LONG PANORAMIC SHOT - LATE
AFTERNOON (LONE**

ROCK, LAKE POWELL)
We are looking at a lifeless desert of sandstone buttes and pinnacles.
There is no sign of vegetation anywhere. CAMERA PANS DOWN to a body of water
that could be the bay of an inland sea. The deep blue of the
sea contrasts sharply to the red sands of the shoreline. CAMERA HOLDS
on the stricken spaceship, wallowing like a beached whale a hundred
yards offshore. The portholes of the craft are beneath the water, and
only its roof and the tail fin of its tail assembly are visible. The
red-hot skin of the ship vaporizes the water around it.
Suddenly a snorkel-like tube sprouts from the escape hatch, which is located amidships.

INT. CABIN - CLOSE ON CLOSED ESCAPE HATCH
Dodge, standing halfway up the ladder. , has fastened a kit of gauges to the end of the
snorkel tube. He reads the dials, removes the kit,
sniffs the air in the tube and then, taking a deep breath, announces:

DODGE
It's breathable.

TAYLOR'S VOICE
(o. s.)
Okay! Blow the hatch before we lose auxilliary power.
Dodge reaches for a control mechanism near the escape hatch.

CLOSE ON TAYLOR AND LANDON
The spray of water coming through the ruptured seam is increasing.
The LIGHTS DIM again and the SOUND of the warning signal FADES. While
Landon fiddles with the radio, Taylor tries to get the tape recorder
rolling, but all we hear are scrambled and unintelligible noises.

LANDON
It's no use ... there she goes.

TAYLOR
Forget it. Abandon ship.

WIDER ANGLE - TIM CABIN
The escape hatch is now open. Taylor darts over to the ladder and
passes a folded life raft up to Dodge. When Landon reaches the ladder,
Taylor hands him two neatly packed rucksacks, and Landon climbs through the escape
hatch. Taylor is about to follow with a third
rucksack, then turns and crosses the cabin for a last look at:

THE TWO CLOCKS - FROM TAYLOR'S P. O. V.
Both clocks have stopped: the red needle of the clock labeled SELF
TIME rests on the numeral ; the red needle of the clock marked
EARTH TIME rests on the numeral .

EXT. TOP OF SPACECRAFT - MED. SHOT
Dodge inflates the raft with a cartridge of compressed air and tosses it into the water. He
and Landon jump into the water and climb onto the raft as Taylor emerges from the
hatch, Taylor slips into the water and climbs onto the raft. He and Landon begin to
paddle toward shore, while Dodge immediately opens another kit and takes a sample of
the water.

CLOSE ON THE MEN IN THE RAFT
DODGE
(half to himself)
Briny... twenty-five percent salinity.
Near the saturation point.

LANDON
(looking back)
She's still sinking...

THE SPACESHIP - FROM THEIR P. O. V.
Only the radio antenna and the tip of the tail fin remain visible.

LANDON'S VOICE
(o. s.)
Going ... going...
The craft vanishes beneath the water.

CLOSE ON THE MEN IN THE RAFT
Dodge is still busy with his kit. Landon is still looking back, but
Taylor doesn't bother to turn his head.

LANDON
Gone.

TAYLOR
(flatly)
We're here to stay.

ANOTHER ANGLE - MOVING WITH THE RAFT
They gaze at the forbidding sandstone battlements as they near the

shore.

LANDON
Well? Where are we? Have any notion, skipper?

TAYLOR
(confidently)
We're some three hundred and twenty light years from Earth. On an unnamed planet in orbit around a star in the constellation of Orion.
(looks off at the "sun")
That could be Bellatrix.

THE SUN - FROM THEIR P. O. V.
Low on the horizon, seen through a dense envelope of dust particles.

DODGE'S VOICE
(o. s.)
Too red for Bellatrix.

BACK TO ASTRONAUTS IN RAFT
Landon glances skeptically at Taylor.

LANDON
You didn't have time to check the tapes, so you don't really know, do you?
(as Taylor ignores him)
What went wrong?
(sardonically)
We weren't programmed to land in water.

DODGE
(grinning)
The question, Landon, is not so much where we are as when we are.

TAYLOR
(stands up in raft)
We've had a nice snooze. Let's start earning all our back pay.

WIDER ANGLE - THE BEACH
As the three astronauts step out into shallow water and pull the raft ashore.

TAYLOR
Take your soil test, Dodge. I'll check the equipment.

Dodge moves inland about ten yards, removes a small hand drill from his belt, extends the rod of the drill three feet and begins to take some subsoil samplings. Taylor begins to examine the contents of the three rucksacks. Landon sits down on the beach. , hands around his knees, gazing moodily at the sunken spaceship. During this and succeeding scenes we sense that Dodge's obsession with scientific inquiry leaves him immune to fear: Landon is possibly more courageous and certainly more "human," for he has many fears to control: while
Taylor -- detached, cool and misanthropic -- is something of an enigma.

TAYLOR
(calls Dodge)
Got your sensors?

DODGE
Yo!

TAYLOR
Geiger counter?

DODGE
Yo!

TAYLOR
(taking inventory)
One pistol... twenty-four rounds of ammo. two medical kits. . one camera... one TX.
(loudly to the others)
We've enough food and water for three days.

DODGE
But how long is a day?

TAYLOR
Good question.
(turning)
Landon -- check your communications kit.

ANOTHER ANGLE - FAVORING LANDON
He seems not to have heard.

TAYLOR
(sharply)
Landon! Join the expedition.

LANDON
(rising)
Sorry...
(crossing to his kit)
I was thinking of Stewart. What d'you suppose happened?

TAYLOR
(flatly)
Air leak. Died in her sleep.

LANDON
You don't seem very cut up about it.

TAYLOR
It's a little late for a wake. She's been dead nearly a year.

LANDON
Then we've been away from Earth for eighteen months.

TAYLOR
By our time.
(smiling at Landon)
You've turned gray.
Landon involuntarily touches the gray hair of his temple as Taylor adds lightly:

TAYLOR
Apart from that, you look pretty chipper for a man who's two thousand and thirty one years old.
(casually)
I read the clocks. They bear out Hasslein's hypothesis. We've been away from Earth for two thousand years, give or take a decade.
(pause)
Still can't accept it, huh?

LANDON long pause)
You know it.

TAYLOR
Because time has wiped out everyone and everything you cared for -- they're dust.

LANDON
Prove it. If we can't get back, it's still just a theory.

TAYLOR
It's a fact, Landon. Buy it. You'll sleep better.
Dodge enters scene. A handful of reddish sand dribbles through his fingers.

DODGE
Nothing will grow here ... . there's just a trace of hydrocarbons, and most of the nitrogen is locked into nitrates.

TAYLOR
Any sign of dangerous ionization?

DODGE
No.

TAYLOR
(rising)
Okay. If there's no life here, we've got just seventy-two hours to find it. That's when the groceries run out.
He picks up one of the rucksacks and puts it on. The others follow suit.

DODGE
Which direction?

TAYLOR
(decisively, pointing west)
That way.

DODGE
Any particular reason?

TAYLOR
None at all.
He moves out. Dodge follows. CAMERA PANS with them. They have gone only a few paces when Taylor looks back over his shoulder and halts.

REVERSE ANGLE - FEATURING LANDON
Landon is squatting in the sand, sticking something into the soil.
It is a small American flag, the size of a handkerchief.

REVERSE ANGLE - FEATURING TAYLOR AND DODGE
Mirth bubbles up in Taylor's throat. He explodes with wild laughter.
He is still laughing as they move out.

DISSOLVE TO:
-ADAWN SHOT (GUNSIGHTLOC #)
THE ASTRONAUTS' TREK
They descend from the plateau (Ochre Dunes)

ASTRONAUTS CONTINUE MARCH,
Across the top of the hills there suddenly runs a line of fire (Black
Dunes).

THEY MOVE ACROSS THE TERRAIN
Jagged bolts of lightning flash across the sky, but bring, no rain, and thunder claps sound
like heavy artillery. (Gray Area)

-OUT
QUICK DISSOLVE TO:
ANOTHER PART OF THE CANYON (OCHRE DUNES AREA) - GROUP
SHOT - DAY
Several huge boulders are dislodged, and the three astronauts run. wildly to escape the
falling rocks. When the avalanche ends, they sprawl on the lifeless sands, breathing
heavily and drenched with
sweat, surrounded by enormous boulders. Taylor looks about him.

TAYLOR
Everybody all right?
Murmurs of assent from Dodge and Landon. Taylor rummages through a
limp rucksack, comes up with some empty food cartons,rummages again,
coming up with a cigar butt.

TAYLOR
Water check.
Dodge takes a plastic canteen from another rucksack and inspects it.

DODGE
Eight ounces.
Dodge lies back and looks up at the sky.

DODGE
It doesn't add up. There's a mantle of dust around this planet and yet it's as humid as a
jungle. Thunder and lightning and yet no rain. Cloud cover every night and that strange
luminosity, and yet no moon.
Landon also looks up at the sky.

LANDON

If only we could get a fix.

TAYLOR
(needling him)
What would you learn? I've told you where you are and when you are.

DODGE
(gently)
Taylor -- quit riding him.

TAYLOR
(harshly, to Landon)
You're more than three hundred light years from your precious planet. Your loved ones have been dead and forgotten for twenty centuries. Even if you could get back, they'd think you were something that fell out of a tree.

LANDON
(wearily)
All right --

TAYLOR
There's only one reality left. We're here and it's now. You get ahold of that and hang on tight, or you might as well be dead.

LANDON
(quietly)
I'm prepared to die.
Taylor turns to Dodge, throws up his hands.

TAYLOR
He's prepared to die! Doesn't that make you misty? Chalk up another victory for the human spirit!
Dodge rises and moves off, o. s. , either embarrassed by this colloquy
or unwilling to hear it again. Taylor, cigar clamped between his
teeth, spins toward Landon.

TAYLOR
Straighten me out on something. Why did you come along at all? You volunteered.
Why?
(a beat; no answer)
I'll tell you. They nominated you for the
Big One and you couldn't turn it down. Not without losing your All-American standing

LANDON
(hard)
Climb off me, will you!

TAYLOR
And the glory, don't forget that. There's a life-sized bronze statue of you somewhere.
It's probably turned green by now, and nobody can read the name plate. But never let it
be said we forget our heroes.

LANDON
Taylor. I'm telling you --

TAYLOR
Oh, and one last item. Immortality.
You wanted to go on forever.
(pause)
Well, you damn near made it. Except for
Dodge and me, you've lived longer than anybody. And with Stewart dead, it looks like
we're the last of the strain. You got what you wanted, kid. How does it taste?
Silence. Taylor lies down, spent of his venom, pillowing his head on a rucksack.

LANDON
(softly)
Okay. You read me well enough.
Why can't I read you?

TAYLOR
Don't bother

LANDON
(looking off)
Dodge ... he's not like me at all. But
he makes sense. Held walk naked into a live volcano if he thought he could learn
something no other man knew. I understand why he's here. But you... You're no seeker.
You're negative.

TAYLOR
But I'm not prepared to die.

LANDON
(heatedly)
I'd like to know why not. You thought life on Earth was meaningless. You despised
people. So what did you do? You ran away.

Taylor's eyes are closed. He is silent for a moment. When he speaks,
his tone is soft, reflective.

TAYLOR
No, not quite, Landon. I'm a bit of a seeker myself. But my dreams are a lot emptier
than yours.
(pause)
I can't get rid of the idea that somewhere in the Universe there must be a creature
superior to man.

ANOTHER ANGLE - FEATURING DODGE
who has been wandering around, studying the boulders and the barren soil. Taylor and
Landon can be seen in b. g. Dodge spots something and squats down to examine it.

CLOSEUP - WHAT DODGE SEES:
It is a tiny desert flower, no more than an inch high.

CLOSEUP - DODGE
His eyes light up as he calls:

DODGE
Taylor! Over here!

CLOSE. GROUP SHOT - ANGLING DOWN
as Taylor and Landon hurry over and kneel down on either side of Dodge.
The astronauts hover over the tiny flower like three magi perceiving the infant Deliverer.

DODGE
Life.
He digs gently around the roots of the plant with a small instrument.

DODGE
Where there's one there's another. And another. And another.

TAYLOR
Let's find them all.

-ASUNSET SHOT
**END OF THE TREK AS THE ASTRONAUTS START FROM THE CANYON
TO THE TAMARISK AREA**
Absolute desolation (Ochre Area). The astronauts start down the canyon.

ASTRONAUTS CAST HUGE SHADOWS

As they move across the terrain (top of Crazy Canyon).

-AJUMP SHOT
As they jump across a gap. Thunder and lightning again (top of
Crazy Canyon).

-BTHEY MOVE DOWN
They march across Crazy Canyon overlook.

-CREACTION SHOTS OF ASTRONAUTS
-

**A-RSERIES OF SHOTS OF DESCENT OF ASTRONAUTS DOWN SHEER FACE
OF A CANYON**
(Wire Grass Canyon).
For a brief moment several "creatures" appear. We cannot identify the species.

QUICK DISSOLVE T:
EXT. A DRY WASH - CLOSE GROUP SHOT - DAY
Blooming tamarisks border a. dry stream bed. Taylor and Landon hover over Dodge,
who is probing the soil with his drill. Their dungarees and faces are caked with dust.

DODGE
It's a stream bed. , no doubt about it -- but bone dry.
Landon strightens up and looks off, startled by something he sees.

LANDON
Look...

LONG SHOT - A CLIFF BEYOND THE TAMARISKS
with the astronauts in f. g. In the distance, on the skyline, we can
make out a long row of wooden crosses. Some animal or vegetable matter appears to be
tied to the crosses.

LANDON
Scarecrows?

TAYLOR
Let's take a look.
Taylor plunges into the thicket of tamarisks, followed by Dodge and
Landon. Their view of the cliff is momentarily obscured. CAMERA HOLDS on the
distant crosses. For an instant only, three "creatures" again appear on the skyline near the
crosses. Then they vanish.

REVERSE ANGLE - THE ASTRONAUTS
as they emerge from the tamarisk thicket-nearer to the base of the- cliff. They halt and look up at:

THE CROSSES - ANGLING UP - FROM ASTRONAUT'S P. O. V.
We can now see the pelts of unrecognizable animals have been bound to the crosses and, thus mounted in a long row, seem to make a boundary or serve as a warning. The living bipeds are no longer visible.

BACK TO THE ASTRONAUTS
Dodge and Landon are still looking up at the strange crosses, but
Taylor is scanning the terrain at the base of the cliff. The sound of rushing water can be heard.

TAYLOR
(half to himself)
Never mind the scarecrows.
He breaks into a run, CAMERA PANNING with him as he moves toward a declivity in the face of the cliff.

MOVING SHOT - DODGE AND LANDON
Agonized with thirst, they follow Taylor.

FLASH SHOT - THE TOP OF THE CLIFF
For an instant we see the bipeds again, moving in the same direction.

EXT. A DECLIVITY IN THE CLIFF - FEATURING TAYLOR
He scrambles up a rock-strewn gorge and looks off at the terrain beyond.

EXT. A WATERFALL - FROM TAYLOR'S P. O. V.
The cascade is not spectacular, but the vegetation around it is startlingly lush. (This location is not at Lake Powell, but at the
Ranch).

CLOSEUP - TAYLOR
His parched lips break into a smile.

QUICK DISSOLVE TO:
EXT. WATERFALL AND POOL - FULL SHOT - DAY
The cascade has formed a cool and inviting pool. Thick foliage grows to its very edge. Dodge is on his hands and knees, testing the liquid with his kit. The others wait expectantly.

DODGE
It's loaded with minerals, but safe.
Without further ado Landon ducks his face into the pool. Dodge scoops up water in his hands and drinks. Taylorfollows suit.

LANDON
(coming up for air)
Can we take a dip?

TAYLOR
(looks around)
Okay.
Landon and Dodge immediately remove their boots, strip down and plunge into the pool. But Taylor does not yet disrobe. Alert and curious, he strolls along the bank of the pool, looking around.

DODGE AND LANDON SWIMMNG
TAYLOR
as he briefly looks around, then starts taking off his shirt.

DODGE AND LANDON
as they arrive at opposite shore.

MED . SHOT - FAR SIDE OF POOL
as Landon sees something on shore.

TAYLOR IN WATER
as he swims across.

LANDON'S VOICE
(o. s.)
Hey, Taylor! Look at this --
Dodge and Taylor climb out of the pool and squat beside Landon.

CLOSE SHOT - WHAT THEY SEE:
The print of a large five-toad foot is clearly visible in the wet sand.

GROUP SHOT - THE THREE ASTRONAUTS
Taylor rises and walks slowly toward the underbrush, scanning the ground for other sports.

CUT TO:
THE OTHER SIDE OF THE POOL - FULL PANNING SHOT

Our view of the astronauts beyond the cascade in b. g. is partially obscured by broad-leafed foliage directly in front of CAMERA, which
PANS SLOWLY away from the waterfall and HOLDS on the astronauts' clothing at the edge of the pool. Suddenly and inexplicably a pair of dungarees slithers away into the underbrush. A few seconds pass. Now a pair of bronzed and brawny shoulders fill the SCREEN, blocking our view.

REVERSE ANGLE - CLOSE ON A HUMAN FACE IN HEAVY FOLIAGE
Or is it human? The hair is matted, the face bearded, the jaw prognathous, the orbital rim prominent.

ANOTHER ANGLE - AT EDGE OF POOL
A brown thick-fingered hand appears from behind heavy foliage and plucks at a boot. The boot vanishes.

BACK TO THE ASTRONAUTS - ON OTHER SIDE OF POOL
Dodge is standing near Taylor and looking back at the spot where they left their clothing. Suddenly he seizes Taylor's arm and points silently at the far bank of the pool.

WHAT THEY SEE:
Another pair of dungarees slithers into the underbrush and disappears.

REVERSE ANGLE - FULL PANNING SHOT - THE ASTRONAUTS
Led by Taylor, they dive back into the pool and swim to the other bank.
Emerging from the water, they look around in bewilderment. Taylor makes hand signals to indicate absolute silence and a reconnaissance. The three astronauts fan out and move cautiously into the jungle (or rain forest).

-

EXT. - JUNGLE (OR RAIN FOREST) - SEVERAL SHOTS - MOVING WITH THE
ASTRONAUT'S
Little sunlight penetrates this dense vegetation. These SHOTS are
INTERCUT with:

WHAT THE ASTRONAUTS SEE:
fleeting forms as yet unidentified; trembling foliage; brown shadows against a green backdrop.

EXT. A SMALL CLEARING - FAVORING THE THREE ASTRONAUTS
who stop at the edge of the clearing, startled by

WHAT THEY SEE:

a number of primitive bipeds, male and female, scarcely visible behind trees and bushes on the other side of the clearing -- here a face, there a portion of a head and torso. Throughout this sequence, the   primitives are never seen clearly or at close range.

BACK TO THE ASTIONAUTS
reacting. They speak in whispers.

LANDON
My God. . they look almost human.

DODGE
They -- there's a herd of them.

TAYLOR
Show them we're friendly.
CAMERA PULLS BACK as Taylor advances a few steps into the clearing, extending his empty hands and beaming like a politician.

TAYLOR
(warmly)
Greetings!

REVERSE - THE STRANGE CREATURES - FROM TAYLOR'S P. O. V.
There are perhaps a dozen of them. They shrink back as Taylor advances
-- hostile, frightened or both. We now see that some of them are clutching articles of the astronauts' clothing and equipment. Taylor stops, stares at them glumly.

TAYLOR
No cigar.

LANDON
Try telling them our names.
Taylor grimaces at Landon.

TAYLOR
Well, if we're looking for an icebreaker...
(turning to the creatures)
Listen, folks ... . .
More shrinking back by the frightened primitives.

DODGE
(softly)
I'm afraid they aren't having any.

-OUT
-A SERIES OF FLASH SHOTS - THE JUNGLE (OR RAIN FOREST):
A pistol goes off with a deafening crash, and the primitive creatures scatter in panicky flight. After a while, quiet returns to the jungle.

EXT. A JUNGLE PATH - THE ASTRONAUTS
They examine the remnants of their clothing and equipment and start to don whatever is able to be worn. Taylor puts on what remains of a ripped pair of trousers; Dodge starts to improvise from the remnants of the kit (it is a torn shelter half). Landon, like Taylor, has the remains of his pants.

DODGE
They didn't leave much did they?

LANDON
Shall we follow them?

TAYLOR
Haven't much choice.
As they walk off down the jungle path.

DISSOLVE TO:
EXT. A GROVE OF FRUIT TREES - ESTABLISHING SHOT - DAY
This need not be a cultivated grove. A few trees (peach or apricot or avocado, it matters not) grow wild in a pleasant glade. Nor is the grove extensive. The three astronauts sit under a tree in f. g. ; the primitives sit under a clump, of trees some fifty yards away. Each camp is feeding and warily watching the other. In the distance beyond the fruit trees is an open grassy plain or cultivated field.

THE PRIMITIVES - FROM LANDON'S P. O. V.
They too are sitting under trees, munching fruit. There are no more than a dozen altogether.

BACK TO ASTRONAUTS - CLOSE GROUP SHOT
TAYLOR
Well, at least they haven't tried to bite us.

DODGE
Blessed are the vegetarians.

THE OTHER CAMP - FEATURING A YOUNG WOMAN

Squatting on her haunches, eating fruit, gazing back at Taylor. Her hair is long and black, her skin nut brown, her face hauntingly lovely and hauntingly stupid. This is NOVA.

BACK TO ASTRONAUTS
Landon looks o. s. at the primitives.

LANDON
We got off at the wrong stop.

TAYLOR
You're our optimist Look at the bright side. If that's the best there is around here, in six months we'll be running this planet.

DODGE
(suddenly)
Look...

THE PRIMITIVES - THEIR P. O. V.
They appear to be agitated although neither we nor the astronauts have yet heard or seen any cause for alarm. The primitives get to their feet, sniffing, listening

CLOSE GROUP SHOT - THE ASTRONAUTS
Puzzled and alarmed by the primitives' behavior, they too get to their feet.

LANDON
Think they'll attack us?
Taylor turns, looks back at:

THE DISTANT JUNGLE (OR FOREST)
From which they recently emerged. There is no sign of life.

LONG PANNING SHOT - THE PRIMITIVES
They suddenly run laterally across the grove, heading back toward their jungle. A rumble becomes audibleit is the SOUND of HOOFBEATS.

VERY LONG SHOT - THE JUNGLE (OR FOREST)
Twelve "horsemen" suddenly emerge from the trees, riding abreast at a canter, like a squadron of cavalry about to charge. The horses look huge. So do the riders, but at this distance we cannot identify them.

LONG PANNING SHOT - THE PRIMITIVES

Cut off from their natural habitat, they reverse direction and flee toward the tall grasses of the savanna (or cultivated field).

LONG SHOT - THE RIDERS
With an exultant battle cry they break into a gallop. The hunt is on.

CLOSE GROUP SHOT - THE THREE ASTRONAUTS
Stupefied, frozen in place.

LONG SHOT - THE RIDERS
Coming closer. We HEAR a rifle shot, then a flurry of shots.

MED. SHOT.
A bullet spanks into the fruit trees above their heads. They run,
CAMERA PANNING with them as they race toward the tall grass in deep b. g.

-A SERIES OF FLASH SHOTS - THE HUNT IN THE SAVANNA
As the "horsemen" close in on the creatures fleeing on foot.

MED. CLOSE SHOT - A RIDER
He reins in, raises his rifle and fires. For the first time, we se that he is a GORILLA. He wears a simple quasi-military uniform -- tunic, trousers and boots.

FLASH SHOT - DODGE
Running through the high grass. He is shot in the back and falls.

FLASH SHOT - TAYLOR
He drops at the side of his fallen comrade.

CLOSE TWO SHOT - ANGLING DOWN ON DODGE
As Taylor rolls him over. Dodge is dead.

WIDER ANGLE SHOT - THE SAVANNA - FEATURING A LINE OF BEATERS
The beaters are all GORILLAS. They carry long sticks and nets, and their task is to flush out the terrified primitives cowering in the tall grass.

-A SERIES OF SHOTS - THE HUNTERS AND THE HUNTED:
(a)Landon flees from one rider only to be cut off by another.
He stumbles and a rearing stallion tramples him.
(b)A third mounted gorilla flings a net over a running female.
She is hopelessly entangled. This is Nova.
(c)Landon lies unconscious on the grassy plain, an ugly gash on his forehead.
(d)Taylor crawls through the tall grass on his hands and knees.

A rider crosses his path without seeing him.

(e)The beaters close in on Taylor, blocking his escape route.

(f)Taylor changes direction and decides to run for it.

EXT, SAVANNA - PANNING WITH TAYLOR

Bent low, he flees through the tall grass. A SHOT rings out. Taylor falls.

CLOSE ON TAYLOR

Lying on his back. His fingers go to his throat. Blood appears between his fingers. He opens his mouth in pain, but no sound comes forth, as
Taylor sinks into unconsciousness.

DISSOLVE TO:

EXT. GROVE - FULL SHOT - THE HUNTERS - DAY

The hunting party has reassembled here beneath the fruit trees. Some of the gorillas have dismounted; others are still on horseback. In the middle distance is a crude horse-drawn wagon. The sides and top of the wagon form a wire cage. Three captive males and one female are visible within the cage. Dodge and Landon are nowhere to be seen. Two gorilla porters enter scene, dragging a male human corpse by the ankles, as two other bearers enter scene with a living burden on a long carrying pole.
Taylor dangles from the pole, held aloft by the bonds around his wrists and ankles. CAMERA PANS with the two gorillas as they dump Taylor into the wagon and close the tail gate.

-OUT

CLOSE ON TAYLOR - WITHIN WAGON CAGE

His throat is smeared with blood. His eyelids flutter as he regains consciousness.

CLOSE SHOT - WHAT TAYLOR SEES:

Three primitive males bound hand and foot. They seem docile in
captivity. The female, Nova, clasps bound wrists around her bound ankles and gazes blankly at Taylor. There is a JOLT of MOVEMENT as the
wagon gets underway

CLOSE ON TAYLOR

With a great effort he raises himself on one elbow and looks out from the cage.

TRUCKING WITH THE WAGON - WHAT TAYLOR SEES:

A gorilla hunter stands over a dead man, one foot planted he chest of his kill and his rifle butt resting on the on   abdomen. Facing him is another gorilla with an old-fashioned camera on a tripod.

APE PHOTOGRAPHER

Smile.
The hunter bares his teeth.

CLOSE ON TAYLOR
He faints.

FADE OUT
FADE IN
INT. A SURGERY - ANGLING DOWN ON TWO OPERATING TABLES NIGHT
The surgery is dimly-lit. (If possible we should be unaware of the source of illumination.) Taylor lies strapped to the nearer table. He appears to be unconscious. The young female captive, Nova, is strapped to the table beside him. She is conscious. Taylor is receiving a direct blood transfusion from her.
Hovering over Taylor are a NURSE and a surgeon named GALEN. Both are chimpanzees. Galen wears a bloody surgical apron, the nurse a white smock. Galen is removing a filthy bandage from Taylor's neck. A door behind them opens and DR. ZIRA, an animal psychologist,enters. She, too, is a chimpanzee and wears a smock like the nurse's.

ZIRA

Which one was wearing the strange clothes?

GALEN
Him.
Zira looks down at Taylor.

ZIRA
Will he live?

GALEN
(irritably)
I don't know. This beast lost a lot of blood.
Galen paws through a tray of surgical instruments. The equipment is obsolescent and the room untidy -- like that of a callous small-town veterinarian.

GALEN
(to Nurse)
There's no probe here. Find one!

NURSE
Yes, sir.
She exits. Zira runs a forefinger across a dusty table. Her voice is soft and well-modulated.

ZIRA
This place is dirty, doctor.

GALEN
(defensively)
These animals are dirty, doctor. They stink, and they carry communicable diseases. Why aren't they cleaned up before they're brought here?

CLOSE TWO SHOT - TAYLOR AND NOVA
His eyes come open. Over this we hear:

ZIRA'S VOICE
(o. s.)
You don't sound happy in your work.

GALEN'S VOICE
(o. s.)
I'm nothing more than a vet in this laboratory...
Taylor feebly turns his head and looks at Nova. She returns his gaze with an unchanged empty stare. We sense that Taylor realizes her blood is flowing into his veins. Over this we hear:

GALEN'S VOICE
(o. s.)
You promised to speak to Dr. Zaius about me.

ZIRA'S VOICE
(o. s.)
I did. But you know how he looks down his nose at chimpanzees.
Taylor rolls his eyes toward the apes. Weak as he is,we see his astonishment at hearing them talk.

BACK TO GROUP AROUND OPERATING TABLE
as the Nurse reenters with a probe and hands it to Dr. Galen, who protests to Zira:

GALEN
But the quota system's been abolished!
You made it. Why can't I?

ZIRA
What do you mean, made it? I'm an animal psychologist, that's all. We don't have any authority.

GALEN
You do pretty well when it comes to getting space and equipment.

ZIRA
That's because Dr. Zaius realizes our work has value.

GALEN
Hmph.

ZIRA
The foundations of scientific brain surgery are being laid right here - in studies of cerebral function in these animals.

GALEN
They're still dirty. And their bite is septic. Look at that ...
He shows Zira infected teeth marks on the back of his left hand.

GALEN
(to Nurse)
Hold his head.
The Nurse complies, gripping Taylor's skull with both hands. Galen leans down and begins to probe the throat wound. Taylor passes out.

DISSOLVE TO:
INT. A ROW OF CAGES - ANIMAL LABORATORY - TRACKING SHOT DAY
The cages are no larger than small jail cells. There are four of them.
Bars, not walls, divide the cages, so that all four are visible. Each of the first three cages is occupied by a primitive male. At the moment the first two are quiet -- dozing or scratching apathetically. The third occupant is stolidly regarding a half-dozen brightly colored hollow wooden boxes, or blocks, Of varying sizes and proportions on the floor of his cage. He is trying to stack the boxes in such a way as to reach a banana dangling from a cord twelve feet overhead. He has correctly selected the first two large, sturdy blocks for his tower under the banana -- but the tall third block is too unstable on its small base to support the broad-based fourth block.

-ACLOSE - TAYLOR
Taylor, Looking much stronger, sits on a pile of dirty straw in the fourth cage. There is a clean bandage around his throat. He watches the block-building primitive with contemptous amusement.
Both the third and fourth blocks tumble to the floor when the primitive tries to mount his tower. He stands there, staring dully at the scattered blocks, then up at the unattainable banana.

-BMED. - THELABORATORY
A door at the end of the aisle opens and a gorilla named JULIUS enters, dressed in a keeper's uniform. He quickly closes the door, snatches up a broom, starts sweeping. Julius is obviously late for work. Taylor struggles to his feet, moves to the bars of the cage, tries to call out.

TAYLOR
(soundlessly)
Hey! Hey!
The three other primitives move toward the bars of their cages. Julius barks at them.

JULIUS
Simmer down!
(points at Taylor)
You especially.
The third primitive goes back to stacking his blocks. Julius comes up to Taylor's cage, indicates a like set of blocks strewn across its floor, extends his broom handle to whack the banana overhead.

JULIUS
Better give it a try, stupid. Unless you like going hungry.
He returns to his sweeping. Taylor glowers at him. A moment later, the door at the end of the aisle opens and Dr. Zira enters.

JULIUS
Good morning, Dr. Zira.

ZIRA
Good morning, Julius. How's our patient today?

JULIUS
No change. The minute you open the door, he goes into his act.
She starts down the aisle toward Taylor's cage. He grasps the bars, awaiting her anxiously. As she passes the second cage, the primitive in it shakes the bars, jumps up and down. His tongue is hanging out. Zira smiles, stops, digs into the pocket of her smock.

ZIRA
(playfully)
Well, what do we want this morning? Do we want something? Speak! Come on, speak!
The primitive continues to jump up and down energetically. Zira takes a cube of sugar from her pocket, holds it up for his inspection.

ZIRA
Do we want some sugar, old-timer?
The man eagerly sticks his hand through the bars. She drops the cube in his hands. He jams it into his mouth.

JULIUS
(concerned)
You could get hurt doing that, Doctor.

ZIRA
Don't be silly. He's perfectly tame.
She moves toward Taylor's cage, Julius behind her.

JULIUS
They're all tame until they take a chunk out of you.

CLOSE SHOT - FEATURING TAYLOR - ZIRA AND JULIUS
Taylor starts to open his mouth as Zira comes up to the bars.

ZIRA
Well, Bright Eyes, is our throat feeling better?

TAYLOR
(frantic mouthing)
Listen, listen -- I can speak --
He winces, puts his hand to the bandage.

ZIRA
(sympathetically)
Awww, it still hurts, doesn't it?

JULIUS
See? He keeps pretending he can talk.
Taylor glares at Julius, slams the bars.

TAYLOR
(mouthing)
I'm not pretending! I can talk!
Zira hurriedly takes a pen and notebook from the breast Docket of her smock, starts to scribble.

ZIRA

(excitedly)
Did you see that? It's remarkable!

JULIUS
Huh?

ZIRA
He's trying to form words.

JULIUS
Well, you know what they say.
Human see, human do.
Taylor is staring in silent fascination at the open and notebook. He stops mouthing, points at them.

JULIUS
Now what?
Taylor gestures for Zira to come closer to the bars.

ZIRA
He seems to want something.
She advances tentatively toward the cage.

JULIUS
I'd be careful, doctor.
Taylor suddenly reaches through the bars, tries to snatch the pen and notebook from Zira. Julius instantly jabs his broom handle through the bars, hitting Taylor in the ribs.

JULIUS
What did I tell you!
(to Taylor)
Try that again, I'll break your arm!
Zira draws back, looking at Taylor in surprise.

CLOSER - TAYLOR
His face is twisted in frustration.

TAYLOR
(mouthing)
What's the matter with you? I can talk! Can't you see that?
Over this a door is heard opening o. s. , and Julius' voice, nervous, deferential:

JULIUS' VOICE

(o. s.)
Good morning, Your Excellency.
Taylor looks o. s.

-OUT
BOOM SHOT - THE THREE APES - FROM TAYLOR'S P. O. V.
Julius and Zira cross to a stout, imposing orangutan who has just entered the laboratory. Julius bows to him. This is DR. ZAIUS. Like the other apes, he wears a simple tunic and trousers, but his garments are of a Costlier material, and several decorations are woven into the sash of his tunic.

ZIRA
(bubbling)
Dr. Zaius, I'm so glad you could come.
He's over here.
Zaius crosses with them to Taylor's cage. Beneath his austere manner, we sense tension, worry. Zira looks up at Taylor, her tone an appeal.

ZIRA
Bright Eyes, show him! Go ahead!
Do your trick!
Taylor just glares at her.

ZIRA
Speak! Go on. Speak again.

TAYLOR
(silent mouthing)
My - name - isn't - Bright Eyes It's
Taylor!

ZIRA
There! Can you believe it? I looks like he's talking.

ZAIUS
(evenly)
Yes, amusing. A man who acts like an ape.
Taylor turns to Zaius.

TAYLOR
(silent mouthing)
I'm not acting! I can talk! How much proof do you want?

ZIRA
(thunderstruck)
Dr. Zaius, I could have sworn he was answering you!

ZAIUS
(nodding, but unmoved)
He shows a definite gift for mimicry.
Zira wiggles her fingers excitedly.

ZIRA
I wonder how held score on a Hopkins manual dexterity test?
Zaius' voice is quiet, but there is steel in it.

ZAIUS
An animal?

JULIUS
Look!
Taylor is frantically wiggling his fingers.

ZIRA
He's moving his fingers!

ZAIUS
Of course. He saw you moving yours.

ZIRA
But perhaps he understood --

-ACLOSE - TAYLOR
He is pleading silently as Zaius' voice is heard over the SHOT.

ZAIUS' VOICE
(o. s. , hard)
Man has no understanding, Dr. Zira.
He can be taught a few simple tricks.
Nothing more.

ZIRA'S VOICE
(o. s.)
I beg to disagree. According to my exper- iments --

-BCLOSE - ZAIUS

A warning burns out of his eyes as he stares at Taylor.

ZAIUS
A word to the wise, Dr. Zira. Experimental brain surgery on these creatures is one thing. I'm all for it.

-CCLOSER - TAYLOR
Fear clouds his eyes. Abruptly, he stops moving his lips.

-DMED. THE GROUP
Zaius sees the effect his words have had on Taylor. He turns to Zira, goes on in a more detached tone.

ZAIUS
But your behavioral studies are another matter entirely. To suggest that we can learn something about simian nature from a study of man is nonsense. Besides, men are a nuisance. They outgrow their own food supply in the forest and migrate to our green belts and ravage our crops.
(looking casually at Taylor)
The sooner they're exterminated, the better.
He turns toward the door. A disappointed Zira follows him. Zaius looks back at Taylor just before going out.

ZAIUS
It's a question of simian survival.

-ECLOSE - TAYLOR
He stares after Zaius, than looks away, slumps to the floor. A pause, then a VOICE is heard.

APE GUARD
Is this the one you wanted, Doctor?

ZIRA'S VOICE
(o. s.)
Yes, thank you.
(pause, her voice much closer)
Bright Eyes?
Taylor looks up.

ZIRA'S VOICE
(o. s.)
I've got a present for you.

-FANOTHER ANGLE - THE CAGE
Standing outside the cage, held on a leash by an APE GUARD is Nova.
She looks at Taylor without expression. Zira gestures at JULIUS.

ZIRA
Put her in with him.
Julius unlocks the cage door-, leads Nova inside, removes her leash and collar. Taylor
has gotten to his feet. Julius goes out, locking the door behind him. Nova hesitates, then
slowly reaches out, takes
Taylor's hand. Zira beams at them.

-OUT
DISSOLVE TO:
EXT. - EXERCISE YARD - ANIMAL COMPOUND - ESTABLISHING SHOT
DAY
It is nothing elaborate, A wire fence encloses a dirt yard. This compound is situated on
the outskirts of Apetown and the town is visible in the distance.
There are about a dozen adult human captives within the enclosure, no more than a third
of them females. Some of them trudge around the dusty yard like convicts in a
penitentiary. Others squat against the sun- drenched wall.
A big male suddenly runs to the fence and tries to climb it. Several guides, armed with
whips and torches, immediately close in on him. The primitive recoils in fear from a
fiery torch and rejoins the captives' circle.

CLOSER ANGLE - THE YARD - FEATURING TAYLOR
He plods sullenly back and forth across the rear of the yard, occasionally glancing off
toward the approaches to the compound. Nova is at his heels. He ignores her. Once again
he looks off, stops suddenly. Nova bumps into him. He turns, impatiently shoos her
away, then looks o. s. , again.

ZIRA AND COMPANION - TAYLOR'S P. O. V.
Zira can be seen approaching with a young chimpanzee, DR. CORNELIUS. He wears a
simple smock over his tunic and trousers. Cornelius glances surreptitiously around,
covertly takes Zira's hand.

CORNELIUS
Do you have to work tonight?

ZIRA
No.

CORNELIUS

Neither do I.
He gives her a quick peck on the cheek.

CLOSER - TAYLOR
He drifts toward the fence, Nova behind him.

MED. SHOT - ZIRA AND CORNELIUS
They come up to the fence. Zira nods toward Taylor.

ZIRA
That's Bright Eyes. The one I was telling you about.

CORNELIUS
What's so special about him?

ZIRA
Watch.
(to Taylor)
Hello, Bright Eyes. How's our throat today?
Taylor stares at her impassively, then looks around to a that no guards are watching, hunkers down, begins to scratch in the dust. Nova extends unclean fingers to touch the bandage on his throat. Taylor flinches, pushes her hand away. Nova touches a bluish bruise on the inside of her own forearm, then searches for a similar bruise on Taylor's forearm.

ZIRA
(excited)
Look -- she remembers.

CORNELIUS
Remembers what?

ZIRA
The blood transfusion.

CORNELIUS
(peeved)
Zira, come on. You know they can't --
(he stops, looking off)
Oh oh. Here comes Number One.
Taylor looks up and o. s. , quickly rises.

ANOTHER ANGLE - THE YARD - FEATURING DR. ZAIUS

Who is approaching the two scientists from deep b. g. Zaius is followed by a huge and much decorated gorilla Whom we recognize as the Leader of the Hunt Club.

ZIRA
(in a whisper, to
Cornelius)
Something's bothering him. He's been prying around the lab for the last two days ...

ZIRA
(as Zaius comes nearer)
Good morning, Dr. Zaius. You know Dr.
Cornelius, my fiance.
Cornelius bows respectfully. Zaius is patronizingly polite.

ZAIUS
Oh, yes -- the young ape with a shovel. I hear you're planning another archeological expedition.

MED. SHOT - TAYLOR
He has stepped back from the marks he made in the-dust, is watching
Zaius with concern.

CORNELIUS' VOICE
(o. s.)
Yes, sir. If the academy agrees.

ZAIUS' VOICE
(o. s.)
The project will require my support, of course.

MED. CLOSE SHOT - ANGLING DOWN ON TAYLOR AND NOVA
A primitive male squats down to see what Taylor has marked on the ground. In letters a foot high he has written:

I CAN WRITE
Nova, at once petulant and playful, erases the WRITE with a bare foot.
Taylor angrily flings her aside. This violence provokes the primitive male, who snarls at Taylor and cuffs him. Over this we HEAR from a distance:

CORNELIUS' VOICE
(o. s.)
I hope I can count on it, sir.

ZAIUS' VOICE
(o. s)
A friendly warning, Cornelius --
when you're digging for artifacts, don't bury your reputation.
Taylor slugs the snarling male, who wades in, trying to bite him.

A VOICE
(o. s.)
Guards!

WIDER ANGLE - THE FIGHT
Two gorilla guards rush in to break up the fight. One of them lashes out with his whip. The other pokes his torch at Taylor. Its flame brushes his arm. Taylor opens his mouth, gives a silent yell of pain, shrinks back. Zira runs to the fence.

ZIRA
(to guards)
Stop! You've hurt him! Take them inside!
Prodding the malcreants with their torches, the two guards herd them toward a doorway in the wall. Zira hurries around the side of the fence and o. s.

MED. SHOT - ZAIUS, CORNELIUS, HUNT CLUB LEADER
ZAIUS
Cornelius, if you have a moment today, I'd like to discuss this expedition of yours in more detail.

CORNELIUS
(eagerly)
Certainly, sir. I'll get my notes and come right over.
He exits hurriedly. The Hunt Club Leader turns to Zaius.

HUNT CLUB LEADER
I don't understand these animal psychologists.
What's Dr. Zira trying to prove?

ZAIUS
That man can be domesticated.
The hunter guffaws. Zaius turns away and looks down at:

THE DUST UNDERFOOT
Just beyond the fence we can make out the letters:

I CAN

Zaius' extended foot appears beneath the bottom wire of the fence. The foot wipes out the letters.

CLOSEUP - ZAIUS
His face is a mask.

INT. TAYLOR'S CAGE - MED. SHOT - DAY
He is slumped against the bars of the cell, gingerly touching a large, reddening blotch on his arm. Julius watches him uncertainly from a few yards away . In the b. g. , the outside door opens and Zira rushes in, hurries down the aisle.

JULIUS
What happened?

ZIRA
Those fools and their torches! Do you have any ointment?

JULIUS
I'll see.
He moves to a cabinet at the other end of the laboratory, rummages through some drawers.

MED. SHOT - ZIRA - FROM TAYLOR'S P. O. V.
Zira comes up to Taylor's cage, studies him solicitously.

ZIRA
I'm sorry, Bright Eyes.

ANOTHER ANGLE - TO INCLUDE TAYLOR
He looks steadily at Zira, who is only an arm's length away. CAMERA
MOVES IN on them. Suddenly Taylor reaches out, snatching the pen and notebook from the pocket of her smock. Zira leaps back with a cry.
Julius grabs a club, races up to the cage, unlocks the door.

JULIUS
I told you what you'd get!

WIDER ANGLE - TO INCLUDE THEM ALL
Taylor is scribbling furiously on a sheet of note paper. The guard moves in, his club upraised.

ZIRA
(pleading)

Julius, don't. It doesn't matter.

Julius swings his-club at Taylor's head. Taylor lifts his right arm to ward off the blow, and the stick strikes him sharply on the hand. He drops the pen and notebook. The guard swings again, driving Taylor to the wall. Then Julius retrieves the stolen articles.

ANOTHER ANGLE - FAVORING ZIRA

The guard returns her pen and notebook with the comment:

JULIUS

Natural born thieves, aren't they?

Zira glances at the notebook. Her face clouds.

INSERT - WHAT SHE READS:

A hasty, almost illegible scrawl:

MY NAME IS TAYLOR.

CLOSEUP - ZIRA

Her eyes afire with a wild surmise.

TWO SHOT - ZIRA AND JULIUS

Her eyes never leave Taylor as she tells the guard:

ZIRA

Get me a collar and leash. I'm taking him to the infirmary.

JULIUS

He's vicious, Doctor. Besides, it's against the rules.

ZIRA

Do as I say.

The guard shrugs and moves Off . . Zira beckons to Taylor. He comes forward to the bars of the cage.

ZIRA

(sotto voce)

You wouldn't hurt me, would you... Taylor?

INT. DR. CORNELIUS' OFFICE - ESTABLISHING SHOT - DAY

The office is simple, almost Spartan. There are books but no bric-a- brac; several painted portraits of Great Apes but no tape recorder or other modern office equipment. Taylor sits at a desk, scribbling furiously on a sheet of paper. His leash has been removed, but not his collar. Zira stands at his elbow. Cornelius paces nervously up and down, reading a sheaf of notes Taylor has already written.

CORNELIUS
(stubbornly)
It's a stunt. Humans don't write.

ZIRA
Dear, you're a scientist. Don't you believe your own eyes?

CORNELIUS
(to Taylor)
Where did you learn to do this?

ANOTHER ANGLE - THE OFFICE
Taylor scribbles something on a small desk pad, rips off the page, hands it to Cornelius.

CORNELIUS
Jefferson Public School, Fort Wayne,
Indiana?
He looks at Taylor narrowly. Taylor nods.

CORNELIUS
(sardonically)
Back on that planet you say you came from?
(Taylor nods again)
Um-hm.
(to Zira)
He may be intelligent, but he's also mad.
Taylor scribbles something else on the pad, hands it to Zira, points at
Cornelius.

ZIRA
(reads aloud)
'And you're a fool'.
She smiles. Cornelius bristles.

CORNELIUS
Now, just a minute --

ZIRA
Oh, Cornelius, be quiet.
Taylor has resumed writing. He hands the sheet to Zira, who reads aloud.

ZIRA

'Dodge was killed in the hunt. What happened to Landon?'
(looking at Taylor)
I don't know.

CORNELIUS
(scornfully)
And they fell out of the sky with you?
Taylor writes quickly, hands the note to Zira.

ZIRA
(reading)
'Not fell -- flew!'
Taylor impatiently begins to fold a sheet of paper.

CORNELIUS
Flight is a scientific impossibility.

ZIRA
And even if it weren't, why fly?
Where would it get you?
Taylor points to the floor and mouths the word "Here. " He flings the paper plane he has just fashioned into the air. It describes a graceful arc around the room and lands at the feet of Cornelius, who slowly picks it up, then exchanges a long glance with Zira.

CORNELIUS
(softly)
Well, now...
Taylor scribbles on a piece of paper, hands it to Zira.

ZIRA
(reading)
'Do you have maps?'
Cornelius puts the paper plane on his desk, crosses to a wall map designed like a window shade. He pulls it down Taylor and Zira join him at the map.

CLOSE ON MAP
It's not a map of the whole planet, of course, but only of that portion known to the apes. Therefore it has the antique and fragmentary aspect of a map drawn by some Babylonian cartographer.
A swatch of blue at the right margin indicates a sea. In the southwest quadrant are the "greenbelts" of the ape civilization, looking on the map like jade stones strung on crescent-shaped necklace. Rubyidots in the lade indicate ape communities. The northwest quadrant, colored brown, is apparently uninhabited. East of the green belts is a

patch of green savanna, and next to it the darker green of a jungle. The eastern quadrants are rendered in yellow, and except for a blue lake, appear to be lifeless desert and barren mountain. This area is marked FORBIDDEN

ZONE.
Using a pointer, Cornelius orients Taylor, indicating a red dot in the middle of the green belt.

CORNELIUS
We are here ...
(moving pointer)
You were captured about here.
Taylor studies the map, then pointing at the lake in the eastern desert, he goes into a brief charade, dramatizing the astronauts' landing and trek.

ZIRA
(interpreting his movements)
You fell in the water here? ... you came ashore ... you marched across the desert ... the mountains ... many days and nights ... and reached the jungle.
Taylor nods, smiles gratefully.

CORNELIUS
(flatly)
Out - of - the - question!.
Taylor slams his fist against the wall in frustration.

ZIRA
(annoyed)
Cornelius, why do you insist on provoking him?

CORNELIUS
(tapping map)
No creature can survive in that part of the Forbidden Zone. I've been there. I've seen it.

WIDER ANGLE - THE THREESOME
Taylor strides to the desk, writes something, hands it to Zira.

ZIRA
(reading)
'Then how do you account for me?,

CORNELIUS
I don't. And I'm not going to try.

ZIRA
But what about your theory? The existence of someone like Taylor might prove it.

CORNELIUS
(shushing her)
Zira, are you trying to get my head cut off?

ZIRA
Don't be foolish. If it's true, they'll have to accept it.

CORNELIUS
No, they won't -
Taylor touches Zira on the arm, makes a gesture of inquiry.

ZIRA
Cornelius has developed a brilliant hypothesis -

CORNELIUS
(quickly)
It's probably wrong --

ZIRA
-- that the ape evolved from a lower order of primate, possibly man. In his trip to the Forbidden Zone he discovered traces of a culture older than recorded time -

CORNELIUS
The evidence was very meager --

ZIRA
You didn't think so then.

CORNELIUS
That was before Dr. Zaius and half the
Academy said the idea was heresy.

ZIRA
How can scientific truth be heresy? What if Taylor is exactly the proof you needed?
A mutation. A missing link between the unevolved primate and the ape -
Taylor bangs his fist on the desk, mouths the word "No!" scribbles something on a piece
of paper.

CORNELIUS

He's touchy, isn't he?
Taylor thrusts the sheet at Zira, who reads it aloud.

ZIRA
'I am not a missing link. '

CORNELIUS
Because if he is a missing link, it means the Sacred Scrolls aren't worth their parchment.

ZIRA
Well, maybe they're not.

CORNELIUS
No, thank you'. I won't get into that battle.

ZIRA
Oh, Cornelius, show some strength!

CORNELIUS
Zira, listen to me. We've got a fine future ahead of us. Marriage. Stimulating careers. I'm up for a raise --
At that moment there is a. loud RAP at the door o. s. All turn.

REVERSE ANGLE - TO INCLUDE THE DOOR
Dr. Zaius enters with another portly figure, DR. MAXIMUS. Like Zaius. ,
Maximus is an orangutan.

CORNELIUS
(flustered)
Dr. Zaius --

ZAIUS
(not unkindly)
Did you forget our appointment,
Cornelius?

CORNELIUS
Oh. , no. , sir. I was just assembling my notes.

ZAIUS
You know Dr. Maximus, our Commissioner for Animal Affairs?

CORNELIUS

Certainly, sir. It's a pleasure to see you again.
He hurries to his desk, starts gathering papers. Maximus notes Taylor with distaste.

MAXIMUS
What is that?

ZIRA
A man, Dr. Maximus.

MAXIMUS
I know it's a man. And you know the rules. No animals outside the compound, and most certainly not without a leash.

ANOTHER ANGLE - THE OFFICE - FAVORING ZAIUS
During the ensuing exchange, Zaius wanders idly through the office. He glances at the scattered handwritten notes, but does not read them.
Meanwhile a rattled Zira replies to Maximus.

ZIRA
Yes, Sir. But this -- creature is a special case.

MAXIMUS
Why special?

ZIRA
We're -- conducting a new experiment.

ZAIUS
Wouldn't it more properly be done in your office?

ZIRA
Yes, Sir.

MAXIMUS
(calling)
Guards?
The gorilla GUARDS enter from outside.

MAXIMUS
Return this beast to the compound.

ANOTHER ANGLE - FAVORING TAYLOR

He regards the apes with hostility as they cross to him. One picks up his leash. Over THE SHOT we hear:

ZAIUS' VOICE
(o. s.)
What's this?

REVERSE ANGLE - FEATURING ZAIUS
Zira stiffens, looking at Zaius. He is holding the paper plane fashioned by Taylor.

ZIRA
A toy. It floats on the air.
(faint defiance)
Try it.

CORNELIUS
(a warning)
Zira... .
Zaius looks down at the paper plane in his hand, then back to Zira. He smiles tolerantly.

ZAIUS
Nonsense.
He crumples the paper plane into a b all. , drops it on the desk. The ape hooks the leash to Taylor's collar, starts leading him out. Zira follows them.

DISSOLVE TO:
INT. CAGES - ANIMAL COMPOUND - FULL SHOT - DAY
The caged primitives are asleep. Julius, the keeper, dozes in a chair outside Taylor's cage. CAMERA PIVOTS MOVING IN ON Taylor, who is lying on his side, also asleep. Nova is curled up behind him. At the sound of a door opening, she comes instantly awake, sitting up and clutching
Taylor's arm. He comes groggily awake, raising his head in time to hear:

JULIUS' VOICE
(o. s.)
What's up, Lieutenant?

REVERSE ANGLE - WHAT TAYLOR SEES:
TWO GORILLA OFFICERS have just entered the compound. They wear side arms. Julius has just risen from his chair.

APE LIEUTENANT
We're taking Number Four over to surgery in five minutes. Have him ready.

JULIUS
How come? The beast's throat is nearly healed.

LIEUTENANT
(snickering)
It's not his throat this time. The vet's going to geld him.

CLOSEUP - TAYLOR
He stiffens but does not move. The apes, of course, speak freely in front of him,
believing the animal cannot understand.

JULIUS' VOICE
(o. s.)
Dr. Zira won't like it. She wants this pair to mate.

BACK TO THE APES - FROM TAYLOR'S P. O. V.
As the Lieutenant replies:

LIEUTENANT
These orders came from Dr. Zaius himself.
There's nothing she can do about it.
The two gorillas exit. The guard crosses to a wall peg for a collar and
'Leash.

CLOSE TWO SHOT - TAYLOR AND NOVA
Pushing Nova aside, Taylor rises.

MED. SHOT - THE CAGE
As Julius unlocks the door and cautiously approaches Taylor, carrying the collar and
leash.

JULIUS
(murmuring)
If only you knew, Bright Eyes, what they're going to do ...
(raising collar)
Stand still now... don't give me any trouble.
The heel of Taylor's right palm crashes into the keeper's, chin, nearly snapping his neck.
Julius falls unconscious. Taylor leans over him, taking his night stick and a set of keys
on his belt.

REVERSE ANGLE - TO INCLUDE NOVA AND MALE IN ADJACENT CAGE

The male has awakened. He stares stupidly at Taylor. Nova is whimpering, little strange cries of fear. Taylor moves o. s.

ANOTHER ANGLE - PANNING WITH TAYLOR
He leaves the cage, moves swiftly to the nearby door and exits.

INT. A DARK CORRIDOR - FULL SHOT - DAY
Barefoot, Taylor silently pads down the corridor to a locked door.

CLOSE ON A DOOR
Which is visible because of a beam of sunlight from the half-open door
of a guard room. We HEAR a murmur of ape voices and LAUGHTER. Taylor fumbles
with the keys, finds one that fits the lock and opens the door.

EXT. ANIMAL COMPOUND - MED. SHOT - TAYLOR - DAY
He emerges, quietly locking the door behind him. Two tethered horses can be seen in deep b. g. , and another gust of LAUGHTER can be heard from the nearby guard room. Taylor looks off.

LONG SHOT - WHAT TAYLOR SEES:
As already established, the animal compound is situated on the outskirts of the apes' community. The strange skyline of the town can be seen in the distance.

PANNING WITH TAYLOR
He starts to cross an open field outside the compound. At that moment we HEAR a shrill police WHISTLE from the guard room. Taylor breaks into a run.

REVERSE ANGLE - THE COMPOUND
As the two gorilla officers emerge from the building and run toward their horses.

EXT. A DIRT ROAD - LONG SHOT - TAYLOR
He runs down the road, starts across the long causeway that bisects a small lake, looking over his shoulder.

QUICK DISSOLVE TO:
EXT. APETOWN - LONG ESTABLISHING SHOT - DAY
The community we sue at the end of the causeway is small and arcane.
There are no power lines, no street lamps -- indeed, no streets as such, but only a small cluster of buildings around a pleasant mall. The architecture of the buildings is faintly derivative of the simpler and less rococo work of Antonio Gaudi -- columns and pillars of brick or
exterior masonry look like the trunks and branches of great trees and suggest an arboreal past.

A small number of apes are visible on the mall:
Taylor darts behind the buttress of a building, casing the situation.
He looks back at:

EXT. LAKE AND CAUSEWAY - LONG SHOT - MORNING
The two mounted gorilla-police can be seen on the causeway, galloping straight toward
CAMERA. It is evident they will soon spot Taylor.

BACK TO TAYLOR - CLOSE SHOT
He retreats from the buttress to a dark archway and vanishes inside the building.

INT. A DARK VESTIBULE - MOVING WITH TAYLOR
The vestibule is nothing, no set required, a dark space through which
Taylor moves toward a shaft of light. We HEAR faintly the discordant chords of an
organ. Or is it an organ? At any rate,a strange and melancholy tune. Taylor arrives at a
font.

INT. A TEMPLE - PANNING WITH TAYLOR
He appears out of darkness into half-light. The rear of the temple is obscure. Taylor darts
behind a screen. Crouching there, he observes:

A FUNERAL CEREMONY IN THE TEMPLE - MED. LONG SHOT
The temple itself is small and austere. There is no altar, but against a plain backdrop we
see a statue of the Lawgiver, a Great Ape holding a book. Below the Lawgiver is an
ORANGUTAN MINISTER clothed in black robes. He stands in front of a closed coffin.
A dozen mourners, seated on comfortable wicker chairs, form a semi-circle around the
coffin. The ape ladies wear cowls.

MINISTER
Weep if you must, but make an end of sorrow. He lives again. Yes, he has found peace
in Heaven.

CLOSEUP - TAYLOR
Crouching, listening, wide-eyed.

MINISTER'S VOICE
(o. s.)
He was a model for us all, a gorilla to remember; hunter, warrior, defender of the Faith.

BACK TO FUNERAL CEREMONY - FROM TAYLOR'S P. O. V.
As the minister continues his eulogy, a small ape boy detaches himself
(as children will) from the group of mourners and comes marching up the aisle toward
the rear of the temple.

MINISTER
Cherished husband, beloved father, generous master -- yes, he was a font of simian
kindness.

REVERSE ANGLE - SHOOTING AT TAYLOR
Who is still crouching behind the screen in deep b. g. The small fry is coming closer.
Over this we hear:

MINISTER'S VOICE
(o. s.)
The dear departed once said to me:
'I never met an ape I didn't like'...
The small fry spots Taylor.

CHILD
(shrill soprano)
Look!. It's a man!
The mourners' heads turn. Taylor slinks toward the vestibule.

ANOTHER ANGLE - FEATURING THE MINISTER
He is aghast.

MINISTER
In Heaven's name ...
(aside to ushers)
Get rid of that creature.
Two ushers rise, moving past CAMERA and o. s.

EXT. TEMPLE - CLOSE ON VESTIBULE DOOR
Staying close on the temple wall, Taylor moves stealthily away from the vestibule door.
The two ape ushers appear.

FIRST USHER
(pointing)
There he is:
They move toward Taylor.

FLASH SHOT - TAYLOR
He runs out onto the mall.

FULL SHOT - THE MALL
Taylor belatedly sees that he is running straight toward his two

mounted pursuers. Darting off in another direction, he races past startled pedestrians.

REACTION SHOT - TWO CHIMP PEDESTRIANS
They do a slow take.

FIRST CHIMP
You see what I saw?

SECOND CHIMP
Must've escaped from the zoo.

MED. SHOT - A MOUNTED COP
He has spotted Taylor. Drawing a folded net from his saddlebag, he swings it overhead (like a cowboy with a lariat) and gallops off in pursuit of the man.

-SEVERAL SHOTS - TAYLOR AND PURSUING MOUNTIE
Taylor runs frantically from building to building, rounding corners, vanishing momentarily and reappearing on another part of the mall. At one point the mountie nearly overtakes him and flings his net, which falls short. Taylor runs on.

EXT. AN AMPHITHEATER - LOW ANGLE SHOT (FROM GROUND LEVEL)
It is an open-air structure, like a Greek theater, located near the central mail. Steeply tiered, it seats no more than fifty apes. The dais in the pit is some fifteen feet above ground level.
Taylor enters scene, running toward the amphitheater. Changing direction, he darts into what appears to be an access tunnel. A moment later the pursuing cop rides into' scene, dismounts and walks toward the amphitheater, looking around for Taylor.

EXT. AMPHITHEATER - HIGH ANGLE SHOT (FROM TOPMOST TIER)
Taylor suddenly emerges from the access tunnel and runs up a ramp encircling the amphitheater. (A retaining wall shields him from the view of the apes.) Pausing for breath at the top of the ramp, Taylor crouches behind the uppermost tier of seats and peers down:

THE AMPHITHEATER - FROM TAYLOR'S P. O. V.
The cop looks around, spots Taylor at the top tier, and starts up after him.

-OUT
EXT. TOP OF AMPHITHEATER - PANNING WITH TAYLOR
He starts to run back down the ramp, but is suddenly confronted by his original pursuer (the dismounted cop coming up the ramp. Reversing direction, Taylor runs around the rim of the amphitheater and vanishes into an exit tunnel. The cop blows his whistle, summoning another cop, who joins him in the chase.

-ANOTHER PART OF THE MALL - A SWIFT SEQUENCE OF SHOTS
In which we see the fugitive, his pursuers and the reactions of ape shoppers and workers.

-EXT. OPEN-AIR MARKET - SEVERAL SHOTS
A market has been set up on one side of the mall, where street vendors behind carts or tables hawk their wares: fruits, vegetables, wearing apparel, etc. As Taylor runs frantically through the market place, several apes join the chase. In the ensuing pandemonium, like the proverbial Chinese fire drill, several tables are overturned.

EXT. A BUILDING - CLOSE ON AN ARCHWAY
Taylor runs into scene, pauses, panting, and looks back at his pursuers. Then he darts through the archway into the building.

INT. BUILDING - TRACKING WITH TAYLOR - DAY
For the moment he is the sole visitor in this wing. His pace slows to a walk as he and we observe fleetingly the specimens in what is a simian museum: Possibly several stuffed and unfamiliar animals; primitive artifacts and fossils; possibly the skeleton of a dog, a cat, etc. Over this we hear a shrill police WHISTLE.

FLASH SHOT - TAYLOR
He runs again.

MED. SHOT - AN APE MOTHER AND CHILD
Looking at the stuffed animals as Taylor races past. The mother gives a startled SCREAM.

REACTION SHOT - A MUSEUM GUARD
He starts after the fugitive.

ANOTHER PART OF THE MUSEUM - FEATURING TAYLOR
He runs past displays of other stuffed animals toward CAMERA and halts abruptly in close f. g. , shocked by:

WHAT HE SEES: DODGE
stuffed and mounted, Dodge bares his teeth at the world.

CLOSEUP - TAYLOR
Reacting in horror. He hears another police WHISTLE and the echoing FOOTSTEPS of approaching guards, which mufffle his strangled gasp:

TAYLOR
Dodge ...

Taylor vanishes in a BLUR of movement.

CUT TO:
EXT. THE MALL - APETOWN - FULL SHOT FROM ON HIGH - DAY
Order has been restored in the open-air market. Taylor bursts suddenly into view from a building on the far side of the mall, running in panic from ape guards in close pursuit. A mounted policeman spots him and   heads him off. Changing direction, Taylor is intercepted by another mounted Gorilla. And then a third.
CAMERA HOLDS, ANGLING DOWN on the center of the mall. We are witnessing a hideous game: "baiting the man. " The mounted police do not shoot or club Taylor, for he cannot escape -- but they circle him, their long whips CRACKING over his head.

CLOSER ANGLE - THE CIRCLE AROUND TAYLOR - FAVORING A MOUNTIE
who unfolds his net, swings it overhead and flings it at Taylor. This time he bags his quarry. Taylor gives up. Spent, docile, entangled in the net, he stands stock-still in the center of the mall. Guards and civillians on foot join the circle around the man at bay. They regard him warily.

CLOSE SHOT - DR. ZIRA
She pushes through the simian crowd around Taylor and hurries to his side.

CLOSE TWO SHOT - TAYLOR AND ZIRA
She paws at the net, crying impulsively:

ZIRA
Taylor, why'd you run away?
Zira removes the net from his face. Panting with exhaustion, Taylor flicks a wild glance at her. He looks demented.

WIDER ANGLE - TO INCLUDE TWO GORILLA OFFICERS
who approach Taylor and Zira. (They are the same gorillas introduced in
Scene .) One of them carries a collar and leash. The other presents an I. D. card to Zira.

LIEUTENANT
Security police.

ZIRA
(promptly)
I'm in charge of this man.

LIEUTENANT
No longer, madame. He is now in the custody of the Ministry of Science.

His colleague moves toward Taylor with a muzzle.

CLOSE SHOT - FEATURING TAYLOR
He speaks at last, his voice hoarse but audible.

TAYLOR
Get away from me, you dirty ape!

FULL SHOT - THE SIMIANS AROUND TAYLOR
The arresting officer steps back involuntarily. All the apes freeze, staring at the speaking animal with mute astonishment as we:

FADE OUT
FADE IN
INT. CAGES - CLOSE SHOT - TAYLOR AND NOVA - DAY
The compound is dimly lit. Taylor, the bandage now gone from his throat, is back in his old cage. The other cages, however, are empty -- their occupants presumably having been moved to the surgery or the zoo.
He is seated on a pile of straw in the rear corner, Nova's head cradled on his lap. Idly he strokes her coarse hair. There is a dull glow of madness in his eyes, and his manner is one of abstract soliloquy, like a man talking to a dog.

TAYLOR
... and that's when I decided to take up astronautical engineering. , you see. I was halfway through college and I...
(he breaks off)
It's an old trick! The silent treatment.
Four weeks and three days, and not a word from anyone. Not Zira. ,or Cornelius... or that damn Julius. No one'll listen... only you. You... Nova. NO-VAH.
His manner is now more direct, and educative. , but she stares in blank comprehension. She brushes his moving lips with her fingers. He shrugs wryly.

TAYLOR
Yeah... me Tarzan, you Jane. That's all right ... I had a puppy once that never barked. He just licked my hand.
(pause)
He's dead now. They're all dead. Everything...
I think maybe they'll kill me, too. Are they afraid of me? I can't hurt them... but I threaten them somehow. Threaten their faith in simian superiority. Yeah ... you're right. They'll have to kill me.
Faint footsteps are heard o. s. Taylor and Nova look in the direction of the sound. A sudden stream of water shoots through the bars and strikes
Taylor in the chest.

WIDER ANGLE - WHAT THEY SEE:
An ape GUARD has a high pressure hose trained on Taylor. It forces him back toward
the rear of the cage. Julius, whip in hand, unlocks the cage, steps inside. He unlimbers
the whip. , cracks it-'in Nova's direction. She recoils. The jet of water hold Taylor at bay.
Julius grabs Nova, begins to pull her toward the door of the cage. Taylor tries to fight
his way through the water toward Julius.

TAYLOR
Let her alone!
Julius swings the whip. It cracks against Taylor's legs, biting into the skin. Taylor
stumbles, falls to one knee

TAYLOR
Where are you taking her? What are you going to do?
Julius drags and pushes the girl through the door, slamming and locking it behind him.
Taylor, fights through the stream of water, flings himself against the bars.

TAYLOR
(raging)
Take your hands off her, you black monster! You filth!
Julius shoves Nova across the aisle to a cage opposite Taylor's, locks her inside.

TAYLOR
Why are you doing this? Say something, you hairy scum!
Julius gestures toward the ape guard

JULIUS
Turn it off!
The ape guard shuts off the hose.

TAYLOR
Answer me!
Julius strides over to Taylor's cage.

JULIUS
(fiercely)
Shut up! The reason no one'll talk to you is because you're a freak!

TAYLOR
Where's Dr. Zira? Why--?

JULIUS

I said shut up!
He slashes viciously with his whip handle against Taylor's fingers.
Taylor yells in pain. Julius and the ape guard start out of the compound.

TAYLOR
(wildly)
Ape! Apes wearing clothes!
It's a madhouse! A madhouse!
He sinks to the floor as the apes go out.

OUT
FULL SHOT - CAGE
Taylor looks desolately through the bars across to Nova's cage. She eyes him sadly.

TAYLOR
(gently)
Now I don't even have you.
(pause)
Imagine me -- needing someone. Back on
Earth there was nobody. Women, yes.
Lots of them. Love making ithout love.
That's the kind of world it was turning into, with the help of cynics like myself.
So I left it -- because there was no one dear enough to keep me there.
(pause)
Did I tell you about Stewart?
(Looking away)
There was a lovely girl. The most precious cargo we brought along. If human life could
survive here, she was to be the new Eve.
(morosely)
It's probably just as well she didn't live to see this.
He looks at Nova. She stretches her hands through the bars toward him.

TAYLOR
I wonder if it's Love between us.
(looks around, smiles ironically)
What a place to find it.

C-FULL SHOT - THE CAGE
Two gorilla officers enter, carrying torches. (These are the same apes introduced in
Scene .) One carries a double set of manacles. Julius comes to meet them. The
Lieutenant takes the two sets of manacles from the other officer, hands them to Julius,
whispers something. Julius comes over and unlocks the door of Taylor's cage. He
advances to

Taylor, who does not move, bends down and clamps the manacles around each of his ankles. Then he straightens, lifts Taylor's arms, pulls his wrists together, snaps on the cuffs.

D-WIDER ANGLE - THE CAGE
Taylor looks across at Nova, blows her a kiss. Julius leads him out of the cage, takes his leash from a snaps it onto Taylor's collar, hands the other end to the Lieutenant. Nova and Julius watch in silence as
Taylor is led down the aisle and out the door.

-OUT
DISSOLVE TO:
INT. INQUIRY ROOM - ESTABLISHING SHOT - DAY
Taylor, wearing his manacles, is seated at a table in the otherwise deserted chamber. There is an empty chair on either side of him. Across the room stands a dais with three rude, high-backed chairs. There is a small table directly below the dais. A third table stands at right angles to the dais. Taylor looks around the empty room. A door is opened by a gorilla BAILIFF, and Zira and Cornelius come into the room, sit down on each side of Taylor. A moment later, DR. HONORIUS, the
Prosecutor and a CLERK enter, take their seats at the third table.

TAYLOR
(softly)
Where have you been? Why didn't you come to see me?

ZIRA
Shhhh!

TAYLOR
What is this?

ZIRA
A hearing.

CORNELIUS
(hissing)
Be clever. Be quiet,

BAILIFF
All rise!
Everyone gets up as THE PRESIDENT, Dr. Zaius and Dr. Maximus enter and mount the dais. The President takes the center chair; the other two flanking him.

BAILIFF
Be seated.
All sit down.

PRESIDENT
(pounds gavel once)
This ad hoc Tribunal of the National
Academy is now in session. President of the Academy presiding. On my right, Dr.
Maximus, Commissioner for Animal Affairs.
On my left, Dr. Zaius, Minister of Science and Chief Defender of the Faith...
(glancing at Prosecutor)
Appearing for the State, Dr. Honorius,
Deputy Minister of Justice.
Honorius rises and bows.

PRESIDENT
(raps gavel once)
Let it be clear at the outset that all matters pertaining to this inquiry are confidential, and anyone discussing them outside this chamber will be held in contempt of the Tribunal.
(a beat)
You may proceed, Dr. Honorius.

ZIRA
(rising)
By your leave, Mr. President -- the
Tribunal has not yet defined the purpose of this inquiry.
The President appears to be taken aback. He glances at his colleagues.

MAXIMUS
You asked for the opportunity to present your case. Surely you must know why you're here.

ZIRA
My own purpose is to save this exceptional creature from mutilation.

MAXIMUS
(promptly)
And our purpose is to settle custodial and jurisdictional questions concerning this beast, and determine what's to be done with him.

ZIRA
At the very least, this man has the right to know whether there's a charge against him.

HONORIUS
(rising)
Objection. The accused is indeed a man.
Therefore, he has no rights under ape law.

PRESIDENT
Well, Dr. Zira? This is a man, is he not?

CLOSE GROUP SHOT - THE DEFENDANT'S TABLE
Sensing that the President has given them an opening, Zira smiles confidently.

ZIRA

He is unlike any man you have ever seen - as we hope to prove.

PRESIDENT'S VOICE
(o. s.)
Answer the question. Is he a man?

CORNELIUS
(tentatively)
Sir? The question is the point at issue:
Is he a man? Or a deviate? Or a freak of nature?

HONORIUS' VOICE
(o. s.)
Objection!

FULL SHOT - THE INQUIRY ROOM
As the Prosecutor continues:

PRESIDENT
Sustained. In all fairness, Dr. Zira, you must admit the accused is a nonape, and therefore has no rights under ape law.

ZIRA
(rising)
Then why is he called the accused Your
Honors must think him guilty of something.
Honorius seems confounded. Zaius takes over.

ZAIUS
This man is not being tried. He is being disposed of.
(pointing at

Zira and Cornelius)
It is scientific heresy that is actually on trial here.

MAXIMUS
Well put, Dr. Zaius. Let us warn our friends that they endanger their own careers by defending this animal.

CLOSE SHOT - THE DEFENSE
Both Cornelius and Zira appear shaken by this threat. Sensing their predicament, Taylor rises impatiently.

TAYLOR
Then I'll defend myself.

FULL SHOT - THE INQUIRY ROOM
Although the judges and Prosecutor have been told that this man can speak, they react in stunned silence to the first sound of his voice.
Flustered, the President bangs his gavel.

PRESIDENT
Dr. Zira -- tell Bright Eyes to sit down.

TAYLOR
My name is Taylor.
The President refuses to address Taylor directly. Checking a document, he speaks to Zira.

PRESIDENT
It says here that his name is Bright
Eyes. You gave him that name yourself.

TAYLOR
(voice rising)
This hearing is absurd! Let me tell my story...

PRESIDENT
(pounds gavel)
Bailiff! Make the animal be quiet.
The Bailiff quickly crosses to Taylor and shoves him roughly into his chair.

PRESIDENT
State your case, Mr. Prosecutor.

HONORIUS

Learned Judges: My case is simple. It is based on our first Article of Faith: that the Almighty created the ape in his own image; that He gave him a soul and a mind; that He set him apart from the beasts of the jungle, and made him the lord of the planet.

CLOSE GROUP SHOT - THE DEFENDANT'S TABLE

Taylor has begun to write something on a sheet of paper. Zira and Cornelius remain attentive to:

HONORIUS' VOICE

(o. s.)
These sacred truths are self-evident. The proper study of apes is apes. But certain young cynics have chosen to study man - yes, perverted scientists who advance on insidious theory called 'evolution. '

FULL SHOT - THE INQUIRY ROOM

As the Prosecutor continues:

HONORIUS

There is a conspiracy afoot to undermine the very cornerstone of our Faith

PRESIDENT

Come to the point, Dr. Honorius.

HONORIUS

Directly, Mr. President. This wretched man, the accused, is only a pawn in the conspiracy.
We know that he was wounded in the throat at the time of his capture. The State charges that Dr. Zira and a corrupt surgeon named
Galen experimented on this wounded animal, tampering with his brain and throat tissues to create a speaking monster ...

ZIRA

(on her feet)
That�s a lie!

PRESIDENT

(pounding gavel)
Mind your tongue, madame.

ZIRA

Did we create his mind too? Not only can this man speak. He can write. He can reason.

HONORIUS
He can reason? With the Tribunal's permission, let me expose this hoax by direct examination.

PRESIDENT
Proceed. But don't turn this hearing into a farce.
Honorius crosses to the defendant's table and favors Taylor with an evil smile.

HONORIUS
Tell the court, Bright Eyes -- what is the second Article of Faith?

TAYLOR
I admit, I know nothing of your culture.

HONORIUS
Of course he doesn't know our culture - because he cannot think.
(to Taylor)
Tell us why all apes are created equal.

TAYLOR
Some apes, it seems, are more equal than others.

HONORIUS
Ridiculous. That answer is a contradiction in terms. Tell us, Bright Eyes, why do men have no souls? What is the proof that a divine spark exists in the simian brain?

TAYLOR
(hands paper to Zira)
Show this to the President.
Zira moves toward the dais. Honorius returns to his own table.

ZIRA
Since the defendant is forbidden to speak in his own defense, he asks that this statement be read into the record.

PRESIDENT
Read it yourself.

ZIRA
(reading aloud)
'I have come to you from a planet in a different solar system. I am an explorer in space, with no hostile intentions against your civilization. On my planet it was the primate Man who evolved Into a thinking animal, while the apes remained... "

PRESIDENT
(rapping gavel)
Stop right there. Bring me that paper.
Zira crosses to the dais, handing the statement to the President. He glances at it, laughs derisively and passes it to Zaius.

PRESIDENT
(to Zira)
This is a joke in very poor taste.

ZIRA
Is it a joke to seek the truth about this man?

ZAIUS
(glancing at document)
Dr. Zira -- you state here that a ship from outer space sank in an inland sea of our eastern desert.

ZIRA
I do not state it, sir. The prisoner does.

ZAIUS
Do you believe him?

ZIRA
(uneasily)
Like you, I find it difficult.

ZAIUS
But how convenient that the proof of his arrival has vanished?
(glancing again at document)
You also state that Bright Eyes had two intelligent companions at the time of his capture.

ZIRA
This is his assertion.

ZAIUS
Where are they now?

TAYLOR
(blurting it out)

One is in a museum!

PRESIDENT
(pounding gavel)
Dr. Zira! Silence that man!
Returning to her table, Zira gestures to Taylor to remain silent.

ZAIUS
How sad. Stuffed and mounted, eh? Dead men, like sunken ships, can tell no stories.
And his other companion?

ZIRA
He doesn't know.

ZAIUS
Mr. President, I believe the Prosecutor has reassembled all he surviving humans
captured in the hunt along with Bright Eyes.

HONORIUS
That's true, Dr. Zaius. My witnesses -- correction -- my exhibits are on display in the
amphitheater.

PRESIDENT
Very well. I suggest we go and look at them.
The President rises, starts out, followed by the others. Taylor is last, being led on a leash
by the bailiff.

OUT
EXT. AMPHITHEATER - FULL SHOT - DAY
The inquiry group files through a door into the amphitheater. Two APES stand guard
over a number of leashed and nearly naked human beings in the center of the pit below
the dais. There are three primitive males, the female Nova -- and Landon. He is dirty and
bearded, but his hair is cropped close.

CLOSE - TAYLOR
He turns to Zira, his eyes shining with vindication.

TAYLOR
(a whisper)
It's him... Landon.

ZIRA
Which one?

TAYLOR
Second from the left.

FULL SHOT - THE AMPHITHEATER
Zaius glances at the accused.

ZAIUS
Well... do you acknowledge kinship with any of these creatures?

TAYLOR
With one of them.

ZAIUS
Identify him, then. Speak to him.
Taylor moves forward for a few paces, stops.

TAYLOR
Landon?

CLOSER SHOT - FEATURING LANDON - FROM TAYLOR'S P. O. V.
Landon looks catatonic. His face is in shadow

WIDER ANGLE - TO INCLUDE TAYLOR
Stunned by Landon's imbecility.

TAYLOR
John ... it's me, Taylor.
Taylor steps forward to grasp his arm. There is still no response.
Taylor takes Landon's head in his hands and looks at his face. There is a fresh scar running from his forehead to the top of his cranium.

FULL SHOT - THE AMPHITHEATER
As Taylor whirls on Zira.

TAYLOR
You! ... You knew about this?

ZIRA
No, I swear -- I never saw this man before.

TAYLOR
(whirling on Zaius)

You did this to him! You've removed his frontal lobes!

PRESIDENT
Silence!
(turning)
Bailiff, take the prisoner inside!
The bailiff Jerks brutally on Taylor's leash, pulling him toward the door leading under the amphitheater.

INT. INQUIRY ROOM - MED. SHOT - DAY
The bailiff enters, dragging Taylor behind him, shoves him into his chair. Moments later the other apes enter the room. All take their seats but Zaius. Taylor glares at him furiously.

ZAIUS
(calmly)
Mr. President, a word of explanation: the creature in question suffered a skull fracture during the hunt. Two fine veternary surgeons under my direction were able to save his life. But the beast could not speak, of course. Nor will he ever speak
Taylor leaps from his chair, livid with rage, approaches the dais.

TAYLOR
You destroyed his memory! His mind! His identity! And, you want to do the same to me!

PRESIDENT
(pounding gavel)
Bailiff! Stop this outburst! Gag that monstrosity!
The bailiff and a husky guard seize Taylor, who continues shouting:

TAYLOR
You barbarians!
The powerful guard twists Taylor's arms behind his back and the bailiff lashes his wrists together. Then the bailiff gags Taylor. His voice is cut off as the bailiff ties the twisted kerchief around his open mouth.
The guard holds Taylor's leash during the rest of this scene.
Meanwhile, Cornelius has risen to his feet. His tone is firm, but conciliatory.

CORNELIUS
May it please the Tribunal: I for one grant that this being cannot have come from another planet. But this much is certain -- he comes from somewhere in the
Forbidden Zone. He has described the region   to us, and described it accurately, for I have been there.

PRESIDENT
You visited the Forbidden Zone?

CORNELIUS
Why, yes, sir. A year ago. With the special permission of the Academy.

ZAIUS
(to President)
He exceeded his orders. His travel permit was promptly revoked.

CORNELIUS
Yes, sir, so it was -- thanks to you. But not before I discovered evidence of a simian culture that existed long before the Sacred
Scrolls were written ...

HONORIUS
Objection! These remarks are profane and irrelevant.

PRESIDENT
Sustained.
(to Cornelius)
Your archeological theories have no bearing on the disposition of this creature.

ZAIUS
(softly)
Let them talk, Mr President. Let them talk.

ZIRA
(rising)
Sirs: our theories have a bearing on his identity.

PRESIDENT
How so?

ZIRA
Let us assume, as common sense dictates, that the prisoner's story is false. But if he does not come from another planet, then surely he sprang from our own. Yes, sprang.
(a beat)
As an animal psychologist, I have found no physiological defect to explain why humans are mute.

HONORIUS

Objection!

PRESIDENT
Sustained.

ZIRA
(plunging on)
Their speech organs are adequate. The flaw lies not in anatomy but in the brain.

HONORIUS
Objection!

PRESIDENT
Sustained.

ZIRA
(voice rising)
Sustain all objections, but face the truth!
Cornelius has regained his courage. Rising to Zira's support, he points at Taylor.

CORNELIUS
Yes! Behold this marvel, this living paradox, this missing link in an evolutionary chain!

PRESIDENT
(pounding gavel)
Silence!
(Puffing with rage)
You have gone too far.

ZAIUS
(calmly)
There you are, Mr. President. I warned you these two would use this hearing as a forum
for subversion.

MAXIMUS
You were right! The advocates of heresy have revealed themselves.

ZAIUS
Mr. President, I think an indictment is in order.

HONORIUS
(promptly)

Yes, sir. The State charges Doctors Zira and Cornelius with contempt of this Tribunal, malicious mischief and scientific heresy.

PRESIDENT
Be it so ordered. The Tribunal will examine all the evidence presented here and in due time render a verdict on the proposed indictment and on the disposition of the deviate in question.
(pounds gavel once)
This hearing is adjourned.
All rise. The guard drags Taylor from the inquiry room. Zira and
Cornelius stand there, stunned by the entrapment into which Zaius has maneuvered them.

-

OUT
DISSOLVE TO:
INT. A SMALL OFFICE - CLOSE ON DR. ZAIUS - NIGHT
The office is as unadorned and Spartan as that of Cornelius -- in fact, with minor changes in decor, the same set can be used. There are many thick leatherbound books on this scholar's desk. Zaius is reading one of them and taking notes. He looks up as someone KNOCKS at the door.

REVERSE ANGLE - SHOOTING PAST ZAIUS
The two agents push Taylor through the doorway.

ZAIUS
Wait outside.
The officers withdraw, closing the door. Collared, wrists manacled,
Taylor stands facing the desk.

ZAIUS
The verdict is in. At the moment your simian friends -- and sponsors -- are free on bail. But they'll soon be brought to trial for heresy.

ANOTHER ANGLE - FAVORING ZAIUS
who falls silent, as if this were the only news of import. We note at once a change In Zaius' tone and attitude. He no longer treats Taylor like a freak animal, but addresses him as an imaginative adversary who must be intimidated by the threat of terror.

TAYLOR
What about me?

ZAIUS

(offhandedly)
Oh, your case was preordained. In a way, you performed a service for the State ...
(smiling)
Because your hearing made it possible for us to expose Zira and Cornelius.
(a beat)
And now the Tribunal has placed you in my custody for... final disposition. Do you know what that means?

TAYLOR
No.

ZAIUS
Emasculation, to begin with. Then experimental surgery. On the speech centers. On the brain. Ultimately, a kind of living death.
Taylor stiffens but says nothing. Zaius lets this prospect sink in, then continues.

ZAIUS
However, it's within my power to grant
You a reprieve. That is why I summoned you here tonight.
(a beat)
Tell me who and what you really are and where you come from, and no veterinary will touch you.

TAYLOR
I told the truth at that 'hearing'of yours.

ZAIUS
You lied. Where is your tribe?

TAYLOR
My tribe, as you call it, lives on another planet in a distant solar system.

ZAIUS
Then how is it we speak the same language?
(suddenly intense)
Even in your lies, some truth slips through! That mythical community you're supposed to come from -- Fort Wayne'?

TAYLOR
What about it?

ZAIUS
A fort! Unconsciously, you chose a name that was belligerent.

(more calmly)
Where were you nurtured?

TAYLOR
I take it you don't believe the prosecutor's charge -- that I'm a monster created by
Dr. Zira.

ZAIUS
Certainly not. You're a mutant.

TAYLOR
That's exactly what Zira and Cornelius claim. You're talking heresy, doctor.

ZAIUS
(smiling)
Of course.

TAYLOR
(growing bolder)
All right, suppose I am a mutant? Why does the appearance of one mutant send you into
a panic?

ZAIUS
Because you're not unique. There was the one you call Landon --

TAYLOR
Then you admit --

ZAIUS
I admit that where there's one mutant there's probably another. And another. A nest of
them.
Where's your nest, Taylor? Where are your women?

TAYLOR
(pause)
Thank you for calling me Taylor.
(more firmly)
Dr. Zaius, I know who I am. Who are you? How did this upside down civilization ever
get started?

ZAIUS
(strangely calm)
You may well call it upside down, since you occupy its lowest level. And deservedly.

(pause)
The eastern desert has never been explored -- because we've always assumed that no life can exist there.
(a beat)
Save yourself, Taylor. Tell me -- is there another jungle beyond the Forbidden Zone?

TAYLOR
I don't know.

ZAIUS
If you are protecting others of your kind, it will cost you your identity.

TAYLOR
I'm not protecting anybody! That hearing was a farce. What have I done?

ZAIUS
You're a menace! A walking pestilence. I do know who you are, Taylor. As I know that others of your kind must live in the
Forbidden Zone.
(decisively)
You have just six hours to make a full confession. After that I'll employ surgery to obtain one.
(calling off)
Guards!
The two burly security agents open the door and enter.

ZAIUS
Take this creature back to his cage.
The guards seize Taylor, start to shove him toward the doorway. He twists around, faces Zaius.

TAYLOR
All right, you can cut me to pieces. It's within your power.
(with force)
But know this, doctor. You do it because you're afraid of me. You do it from fear!
Zaius jerks his head silently toward the door. The apes drag Taylor through it.

DISSOLVE TO:
INT. ADJACENT CAGES - MED. SHOT - NIGHT
A few hours have passed. Nova is watching Taylor from her cage across the aisle. He sits on the pile of straw. There is an ugly welt on his cheek made by the security officer's whip. FOOTSTEPS are heard. Taylor and Nova look up and off.

REVERSE ANGLE - WHAT THEY SEE:
A solemn, teen-age chimp named LUCIUS appears outside the cage. The guard Julius rises from his chair.

LUCIUS
Are you Julius?

JULIUS
What do you want?

LUCIUS
I'm from the Office of Animal Affairs.
(indicating Taylor)
This male's to be transferred to the zoo.

JULIUS
At this hour? Who says so?
Taylor enters scene, coming over to the cage bars as Lucius continues gravely, with just a note of disdain.

LUCIUS
Don't they tell you anything? The Anti- vivisectionist Society is up in arms. They're going to save this beast from those butchers in the lab. If he can speak he belongs in the public zoo.
(taking off)
But what'll probably happen is that some money-mad grown-up will put him in a circus. And then we'll have to pay to see what rightfully should have --

JULIUS
Stop making speeches and show me the order.
Lucius hands the guard a document. It is dark here, so Julius crosses to a beam of light near the bars and studies the document. Lucius, behind the guard's back, signals frantically for Taylor to seize or strike the guard. Taylor is slow to understand. Lucius shakes his head impatiently.

JULIUS
(peering at document)
This order's no good. It must be counter- signed by Dr. Zaius --
Lucius suddenly gives Julius a violent shove. The guard's head crashes against the bars and he is stunned.

LUCIUS
Hit him!

Taylor complies bringing down the heel of his fist on the nape of the guard's neck. Julius collapses. The youngster immediately squats down, gags him, and begins to bind him hand and foot. CAMERA MOVES IN.

TAYLOR
Who are you?

LUCIUS
(looking up,coolly)
So you can talk.
(as he works)
I'm Dr. Zira's nephew. This abduction was her idea. You're not really going to the zoo. That's just our cover story in case we're stopped.
(off again)
Although I do feel that if it ever came down to a question of whether something like you should be public or private property --

TAYLOR
Come on. Get me out of here.
Taking the guard's keys, Lucius rises and unlocks the cage. Nova enters the scene, coming to the bars of her cage.

CLOSE TWO SHOT - TAYLOR AND NOVA
He gazes at her, tense with indecision. She flashes an imploring smile, a mute appeal that cannot be denied. Over this we hear:

LUCIUS' VOICE
(o. s.)
We've got to move fast.

WIDER ANGLE - TO INCLUDE LUCIUS
as Taylor leaves his cage.

TAYLOR
She comes along too.

LUCIUS
Zira doesn't want your female.

TAYLOR
I want her.

LUCIUS

(a shrug)
If you insist. But I'm not taking any orders --

TAYLOR
Fine. Just let her out.
Lucius unlocks Nova's cage. She comes out quickly, takes Taylor's hand.
They follow Lucius out of the compound.

EXT. ANIMAL COMPOUND - MED. SHOT - NIGHT
A horse-drawn caged wagon (like that used in the hunt) stands near the building. Zira waits at the rear of the wagon. Lucius, Taylor and Nova emerge from a doorway or archway and join her. Zira notes Nova's
presence with disapproval. They speak in undertones.

ZIRA
(to Lucius)
I told you not to bring the other one.

LUCIUS
He wouldn't leave her.

ZIRA
(with a sigh)
All right...
(to the humans)
Get in... hurry. Put this on.

TAYLOR
Listen-

ZIRA
Taylor -- just keep quiet and we may get away with this. Remember that men all look alike to most apes.
Taylor and Nova comply, climbing into the cage. Lucius closes the tailgate. Lucius and Zira move to the front of the wagon and climb aboard. Lucius takes the reins. As they move off:

WIPE TO:
EXT. LAKE AND CAUSEWAY - LONG HIGH ANGLE SHOT - NIGHT
As previously established, the animal compound is on the outskirts of
Apetown. The abductors must cross the causeway on their route of escape. In the distance, near the gazebo, we can see the lights of several torches.

The caged wagon rolls into scene and out onto the causeway. At the same time a mounted gorilla leading two pack animals appears on the far side of the causeway, coming toward CAMERA. Lucius stops the wagon.

CLOSE TWO SHOT - LUCIUS AND ZIRA - ON THE WAGON
LUCIUS
(apprehensively)
Gorilla hunters ...

ZIRA
Keep moving. We can't turn back now.

BOOM SHOT - THE CAUSEWAY
As the mounted hunter nears the wagon, we can see two bodies slung across the backs of the pack animals.

FLASH SHOT - TAYLOR AND NOVA - IN WAGON CAGE
They look out at:

THE PASSING HORSES - FROM THEIR P. O. V.
The bodies on the horses are naked human corpses.

MED. LONG SHOT - THE CAUSEWAY - REVERSE ANGLE
In immediate f. g. , near the gazebo, is a similar wagon. It has lost a wheel, and its rear axle lies on the edge of the causeway. Two naked primitive males can be dimly seen within the cage. Four or five armed gorilla hunters stand near the wagon: two of them carry torches; the others are passing a jug from hand to hand-.
The leader of the Hunt Club, still on horseback, holds up his hand as the lab wagon approaches.

LEADER
Hold it!
Lucius obeys. The hunters on foot swarm around his wagon as their leader calls authoritatively:

LEADER
Ah, Doctor Zira! Our wagon broke down! I'm afraid we'll have to commandeer yours.

CLOSER ANGLE - THE LAB WAGON
as the Hunt Club Leader rides over, recognizing the animal psychologist.

ZIRA

You can't! I've two sick humans in the cage. We're taking them to the chief vet at the zoo ...

LEADER
(indicating his own wagon)
We bagged two live ones today. I'll have to ask you to take them along.
He moves to the rear of the wagon.

ZIRA
(following him; frantically)
No, no, my animals are diseased... Leave them alone! They're diseased, I tell you!
Lucius jumps down and runs toward the rear of the wagon.

REVERSE ANGLE - REAR OF WAGON
The hunters have opened the tailgate and are shining their torches on the humans. They sound ready for sport.

FIRST HUNTER
Give him a taste of fire!
One of the hunters points his torch at Taylor, who, quite naturally, shrinks back as Lucius runs into scene.

LUCIUS
Stand back! He's dangerous!

FIRST HUNTER
Why?

ZIRA
He's rabid! His bite is fatal!

FIRST HUNTER
You serious?

LUCIUS
You would die in agony!
(with appropriate gestures)
Frothing at the mouth!
The hunters fall back. Lucius promptly locks the tailgate and he and
Zira run back to the front of the wagon. Lucius snaps the reins and the wagon moves off.
The hunters follow it a few paces, pausing near their mounted leader.

FIRST HUNTER

They treat those animals better than they treat us.

LEADER
I still say the only good human is a dead human.
The fugitives' wagon recedes beyond the gazebo, as we:

DISSOLVE TO:
EXT. AN OPEN RANGE - LONG SHOT - DAWN
The horse-drawn wagon is silhouetted-against the dawn light, bumping across a semi-arid plain studded with mesquite and sage. (This SCENE can be SHOT either on the Navajo reservation near Page or on the
Ranch).

DISSOLVE TO:
EXT. SAVANNA (OR CULTIVATED FIELDS) - LONG SHOT - MORNING
This is the same area described on page , where the hunt occurred. As the wagon rolls along a dirt track, the tall grasses of the savanna (or cultivated field) can be seen in b. g.

CLOSE TWO SHOT - TAYLOR AND NOVA - IN WAGON CAGE
Taylor is dozing, but the girl is alert and nervous. She peers out at the field, apparently recognizing or remembering this terrain. She nudges Taylor, waking him.

EXT. GROVE OF WILD FRUIT TREES - LONG PANNING SHOT - DAY
This, too, is the location described on page . CAMERA PANS with the wagon as it rolls into the grove and HOLDS on three horses. Cornelius sits astride one horse; the other two nags are heavily burdened with packs and saddlebags.

CLOSER ANGLE - THE GROVE - FAVORING CORNELIUS
He dismounts as Zira and Lucius jump down from the wagon and hurry toward him. Cornelius and his fiancee embrace and kiss lightly, ape-fashion.

CORNELIUS
How did it go?

ZIRA
There was one bad moment -- some hunters stopped us.

LUCIUS
(calmly)
I pursuaded them our beasts had rabies.

CLOSE TWO SHOT - TAYLOR AND NOVA - IN CAGED WAGON

The apes discussing the abduction are out of earshot. Exasperated to be thus ignored and caged, Taylor kicks the tailgate, shouting:

TAYLOR
Let me out of here!

WIDER ANGLE - TO INCLUDE THE GROUP
Lucius hurries back to unlock the tailgate. Taylor gets out of the wagon, stretching his stiffened joints. Nova follows suit. During the ensuing exchange the girl seems strangely agitated, pacing to and fro, her eyes scanning the grove and fields in search of someone or something.

CORNELIUS
(approaching)
Well, Taylor -- we're all fugitives now.

TAYLOR
Do you have any weapons?

CORNELIUS
The best. But we won't need them.

TAYLOR
Just the same, I want one.
He moves toward one of the horses. Cornelius starts after him.

CORNELIUS
Look here, Taylor. I'm in charge of this expedition --
Taylor takes a rifle from one of the packs, examines it.

TAYLOR
Fair enough. But you're no longer in charge of me. And I don't mean to be captured again.
Zira and Lucius have come up.

CORNELIUS
(peeved)
As you wish.

TAYLOR
Zaius seems to think there might be another jungle beyond the Forbidden Zone.
That's what we'll try for. What about you?

ZIRA

Cornelius and I have been indicted for heresy. Unless we can prove our theories, we don't stand a chance of acquittal.

TAYLOR

You're going back to the Forbidden Zone?

CORNELIUS

To the diggings I worked at a year ago.
It's a three day ride across the eastern desert, near where you claim you landed from that planet of yours.

TAYLOR

You still don't believe me, do you?

CORNELIUS

(shrugs)
It's a long detour to Dead Lake. What would we find?
Taylor makes a helpless gesture, realizing that he cannot present sure proof.

TAYLOR

Nothing much. The remnants of a life raft.
Maybe a small flag. The emblem of my countrymen.

CORNELIUS

Sorry, Taylor. The terrain around that lake is poisonous. There is no fresh water, no vegetation. Nothing.

TAYLOR

I know ... Nevertheless, I thank you for saving us. You'll be in trouble for going there.

ZIRA

(a smile)
We've been in trouble since the moment we met you.
Nova seizes Taylor's arm to get his attention. Trying to communicate,
she makes whimpering sounds and points at:

-
OMIT
THE DISTANT JUNGLE - AS SEEN FROM THE GROVE
This is the same view of the jungle that Taylor saw when the gorilla
hunters emerged from the trees. (Page)

ZIRA'S VOICE
(o. s.)
What's she pointing at?

BACK TO TAYLOR AND THE OTHERS
Taylor smiles at Nova, gives her a reassuring shrug.

TAYLOR
That's the way home. And she knows it.
Nova turns away, still holding Taylor's arm, tries to lead him toward the jungle.

TAYLOR
(sharply)
Nova!
(she turns; he shakes his head, says gently)
We can't stay there. It's not safe.
She looks at him sadly.

ZIRA
We'd better get started. If the mounted police pick up our trail, they'll come this far at least.

CORNELIUS
Right.
(to Lucius)
Let's put the water and provisions in the wagon.
He and Lucius move off toward the horses.

ZIRA
(indicating Nova)
Are you going to take her with you?

TAYLOR
Yes.

ZIRA
Actually, you're a different breed.
This creature will never evolve.

TAYLOR
Maybe not.

ZIRA

(smiling)
You want her that much?

TAYLOR
(testily)
You threw us together, remember? And you guessed right. Men, like apes, get despondent without a mate.
He walks off to help Lucius and Cornelius. Nova tags along behind him as we:

DISSOLVE TO:
THE GROUP MOVES ACROSS A PLATEAU
DISSOLVE TO:
EXT. DRY WASH AND TAMARISKS - FEATURING SCARECROWS - DAY
The caravan is crossing, in a reverse direction, the route taken by the astronauts on page . The three apes are on horseback. Taylor and Nova follow in the wagon. They are nearing the row of sinister scarecrows on the bluff above the dry wash.

MED. SHOT - THE THREE MOUNTED APES
They halt briefly and look up at the crosses. Lucius is impressed.

LUCIUS
Who put them up?

ZIRA
The Hunt Club.

LUCIUS
To scare off humans?

CORNELIUS
To scare us, too. We're entering the Forbidden Zone.
They move off again, riding across the dry wash.

TWO SHOT - TAYLOR AND NOVA - SEATED ON THE WAGON
They, too, have stopped and are looking up at the scarecrows. Nova is plainly terrified. She grabs Taylor's arm, whimpers.

TAYLOR
Don't worry. You'll be safe with me.
(sudden smile)
Here. It's time you learned to earn your keep.
He hands the reins to Nova. She just sits there. He demonstrates.

TAYLOR
You can do it. Like this ...
Nova flicks the reins, reacting in wide-eyed, open-mouthed disbelief as the horse obeys
her.

DISSOLVE TO:
EXT. DESERT PLATEAU - LONG HIGH ANGLE SHOT - DAY FOR NIGHT
The party is traversing a red desert to the east of Dead Lake. Great sandstone monoliths
rise from the desert floor. From this vantage point the horses look no bigger than ants.

DISSOLVE TO:
EXT. RIM OF A DEEP GORGE - HELICOPTER SHOT - DAY
This is terrain never before seen in this picture. (Lake Powell location, a few miles
northeast of Wahweap). The party can be seen on the rim of a flat desert tableland that
falls away abruptly to a vast, irregular river of deep blue water. Taylor, Cornelius and
Lucius are unloading the wagon and repacking their provisions and equipment on the
backs of horses. Zira watches them.

CLOSER ANGLE - THE GROUP
Zira wanders off, falls to her knees.

LUCIUS
Something's wrong with your mate.
Taylor looks off. He and the others move quickly to Nova, CAMERA
PANNING with them.

B-CLOSE GROUP SHOT - AROUND NOVA
She has been retching. Taylor lifts her up. She is faint with nausea.
Zira squats down beside them.

ZIRA
Let me handle this.
(ruefully, to Taylor)
You may be smarter than I am, but I'm the veterinary on this planet.
Assisting Nova to her feet, Zira leads her off toward the wagon.

C-MED. SHOT - CORNELIUS, TAYLOR AND LUCIUS.
Taylor watches the departing females, then looks down at the river.

TAYLOR
Where does the river lead?

CORNELIUS

It empties into a sea some miles from here. That's where the cave is.

D-LONG SHOT - THE RIVER - FROM THEIR P. O. V. .
The river winds o. s. between the sheer sandstone Cliffs rising from either bank.

TAYLOR'S VOICE
(o. s.)
And beyond that?

E-THREE SHOT - TAYLOR, LUCIUS AND CORNELIUS
CORNELIUS
Don't know. At high tide you can't ride along the shore, and we had no boats on the last
expedition.

TAYLOR
You've never told me why this region's called the Forbidden Zone.

CORNELIUS
No one really knows. It's an ancient taboo. Set forth in the Sacred Scrolls.
The Lawgiver pronounced the area deadly.

LUCIUS
Shouldn't we be moving on?

TAYLOR
I'm for that.
They start toward the horses and wagon.

F-GROUP SHOT - NEAR WAGON
Zira is looking curiously at Nova, who stands in the shade leaning against the wagon as
the males enter the scene. Nova's nausea has passed, and she comes smiling to Taylor.

TAYLOR
What's the diagnosis, doctor? A touch of the sun?

ZIRA
She's not sick at all.
(a beat)
She's pregnant.

G-CLOSEUP - TAYLOR
Consternation slowly gives way to wonder. He grins.

TAYLOR
So I'm not an altogether different breed, you see?

DISSOLVE TO:
-

THE DESCENT OF THE GORGE - SEVERAL SHOTS - DAY
To reach the camp site -- a beach at the base of the gorge -- the party must lead the horses along a narrow trail that zigzags down the face of the sandstone cliffs. They have abandoned the wagon.

DISSOLVE TO:
EXT. ARCHEOLOGICAL CAMP - ESTABLISHING SHOT - DAY
Sand bars and two narrow beaches are in evidence here. The camp itself consists of several lean-tos against the cliff wall. Above the camp, reached by ladders connected to scaffolding, is the mouth of a cave.
Zira is cleaning up the breakfast things; Zaius and Lucius are sorting out equipment.

CLOSER ANGLE - TAYLOR AND ZIRA
A small bowl of water rests on the ground in front of Taylor He has nearly finished shaving himself with a sharp hunting knife. Nova watches, a look of fascinated approval on her face. Taylor rinses off his knife, starts to dry it. Nova reaches out, gently strokes his smooth -- if nicked -- chin.

TAYLOR
(smiling)
You like it?
Lucius and Cornelius come up, Zira with them.

LUCIUS
(disapprovingly)
Why did you do that? Scrape off your hair?

TAYLOR
In my world -- before I left it - only youngsters of your age wore un- scraped hair.

CORNELIUS
(to Taylor, quizzically)
It makes you look somehow ... less intelligent.
Taylor grins wryly at Cornelius, picks up his rifle.

TAYLOR
When are you going to show me what's in the cave?

CORNELIUS
Right now, if you like.
They cross the beach to the ladders, when suddenly they hear the sound of horses. They look o. s.

B-WHAT THEY SEE:
Dr. Zaius and five armed and mounted apes have come around the corner of the beach and ride toward them through the rocks.

C-MEDIUM - THE GROUP
Taylor scrambles up onto the lower scaffold. Lucius runs to a lean-to, scoops up his rifle.

CORNELIUS
Lucius -- don't fire at them.
The party rides up.

ZAIUS
You're all under arrest!
(to Lucius)
You seditious scoundrel. Drop that rifle.

-OUT
FLASH SHOT - LUCIUS
He wavers, lowering his piece.

WIDER ANGLE - TO INCLUDE BOTH GROUPS
Zaius' gorillas ride forward a few paces, but halt again as Taylor shouts:

TAYLOR
Stop right there.

ZAIUS
Don't be a fool. You're outnumbered and outgunned.
Taylor aims at Zaius and calls out:

TAYLOR
If there's any shooting, Dr. Zaius, you'll be the first to die. Depend on it.

CORNELIUS
(protesting)
Taylor, you're not in command here.
Put down that gun.

TAYLOR
Shut up.
Silence. Zaius knows Taylor isn't bluffing.

ZAIUS
Very well.
(to his followers)
Lower your weapons.
They obey. Taylor calls again:

TAYLOR
(pointing)
Tell them to move around the point.
Out of range.
Zaius turns and whispers to his apes. They rein about and ride away through the rocks.
Zaius dismounts and approaches the fugitives alone.
He is unarmed.

CLOSER ANGLE - THE GROUP
As Zaius draws nearer) Lucius lowers his rifle. But Taylor keeps his at the ready.

CORNELIUS
(uncertainly)
How did you know we'd come here?

ZAIUS
It wasn't difficult. Only an apostate or a lunatic would flee to the Forbidden
Zone.
(a glance at Taylor)
I see you brought along the female of your species.
(Taylor nods)
I didn't realize a man could be monogamous.

TAYLOR
On this planet -- it's easy.
Zaius laughs derisively, then turns to the apes.

ZAIUS
(evenly)
I ask you to reconsider the rash course you've taken. If you're convicted of heresy, the most you'll get is two years. But if you persist in pointing guns in my direction, you'll hang for high treason.

CORNELIUS
(respectfully)
We've never meant to be treasonable, sir.
(pointing off)
But up there, in the face of that Cliff, is a vast cave -- and in that cave a fabulous treasure of fossils and artifacts.

ZAIUS

I've seen some of your fossils and artifacts.
They're worthless.

TAYLOR
(derisively)
And that's your Minister of Science. Honor- bound to expand the frontiers of knowledge.

ZIRA
(worried)
Taylor, please --

TAYLOR
Except that he's also the Chief Defender of the Faith.

ZAIUS
(loftily)
There is no contradiction between faith and science. True science.

TAYLOR
(suddenly angered)
All right, let's see if you're willing to put that statement to a test.

CORNELIUS
Taylor, I'd rather you -

TAYLOR
No. You saved me from this fanatic. Maybe
I can pay you back.

ZAIUS
(calmly)
What is your proposal?

TAYLOR
When were the Sacred Scrolls written?

ZAIUS
Twelve hundred years ago.

TAYLOR
Very well. If Zira and Cornelius can prove that those scrolls don't tell the whole truth of your history; if they can show you   definite evidence of another culture from an unrecorded past -- will you exonerate them?

ZAIUS
Of course.

TAYLOR
Okay. Up to the cave.
He gestures toward the path leading to it. Zaius, Zira, and Cornelius start upward. Lucius starts to follow them.

TAYLOR
Sorry, Lucius. You'll have to stay here and guard the horses.

LUCIUS
Always giving orders. Just like every other adult.

TAYLOR
Relax. You'll see it all later.
He pats the barrel of Lucius' gun, in the manner of a stern but benevolent non-com, then starts up the trail with Nova at his heels.
Lucius, unused to taking commands from an animal, scowls after him, then shrugs, adjusting to the Idea.

-
OUT
EXT. WESTERN WALL OF GORGE - LONG SHOT - ANGLING UP
AFTERNOON
The sun hovers over the lofty rim of the lake like a great red balloon.
The wall of the gorge, in shadow, is a darker hue.

EXT. EASTERN WALL OF GORGE - LONG SHOT - ANGLING UP
The crenelated east wall, looking like a red cathedral, is aglow with sunlight. So is the mouth of the cave as the three apes, Taylor and
Nova pass through it and o. s.

INT. CAVERN - BOOM SHOT - DAY

Nature has formed a vaulted room here. It need not be enormous, but should be as weird and fantastic as production capabilities permit.

There is an ape-made excavation in the floor of the cave, some ten feet square and eight feet deep. Some small objects lie on the rim of the excavation. Zaius, Cornelius, Zira, Taylor and Nova enter from the outside.

(AUTHOR'S NOTE: The effect should be an eyeful. I wish to create an illusion of sunlight penetrating this cave, flooding it with direct, refracted illumination, transforming it into a kaleidoscopic cavern.)

ZAIUS
Present your evidence, Cornelius.

Cornelius clambers down into the pit, followed by Zira. Taylor bends down, examines some of the artifacts lined along the edge of the excavation. Nova sits beside him.

CORNELIUS
(pointing)
It was at this level I discovered traces of an early ape creature -- stage of primitive barbarism, really -- dating back roughly thirteen hundred years. It was here
I found cutting tools and arrowheads of quartz and the fossilized bones of carnivorous gorillas.

CAMERA (ON BOOM) MOVES IN SLOWLY as Cornelius continues:

CORNELIUS
But the artifacts lying at your feet were found here, at this level. And that's the paradox. The more ancient culture is the more advanced. Admittedly, many of these objects are unidentified, but clearly they were fashioned by beings with a knowledge of metallurgy.

CAMERA KEEPS MOVING IN on the group in and around the excavation as
Cornelius continues:

CORNELIUS
Indeed, the very fact that these tools are unknown to us could suggest a culture in certain ways almost equal to our own.
Some of the evidence is uncontestable ...

ZAIUS
(interrupting)
Don't speak to me in absolutes. The evidence is contestable.

CORNELIUS
I apologize.

ZAIUS

To begin with, your methods of dating the past are crude, to say the least. There are geologists on my staff who would laugh at your speculations.

TAYLOR
Perhaps that's why they're on your staff.
Zaius flicks a hostile glance at Taylor, then looks down at the artifacts. He nudges them with his foot.

ZAIUS
Secondly, if these 'tools' as you call them, are unidentified, why are they introduced as 'evidence' of anything?

ZIRA
(promptly)
But there's the doll, sir.

ZAIUS
What?

CORNELIUS
(pointing)
Right there. The human doll.
Zaius deigns to stoop and pick it up.

CLOSE ON DOLL - IN ZAIUS' HAND
It is only a porcelain fragment, but the head is intact, and it is unmistakably the form of a human child.

ZAIUS
What does this prove? My grand- daughter plays with human dolls.

FULL SHOT - THE EXCAVATION - INCLUDING TAYLOR
Exasperated, Zira turns to the man for confirmation.

ZIRA
Taylor! Tell him.

TAYLOR
He has a point. On my planet children often play with ape dolls.
Zaius idly tosses the doll to the ground near Nova. She picks it up, studies it.

GROUP SHOT - THE THREE APES
Cornelius tries again.

CORNELIUS
A doll alone proves nothing. True. But the doll was found beside the jawbone of a man -
- and no trace of simian fossils has turned up in this deposit.

ZAIUS
Your conclusion is premature. Have you forgotten your Scripture? The Thirteenth
Scroll?
(quoting from memory)
'And Proteus brought the upright beast into the garden, and chained him to a tree, and
the children made sport of him. '

CORNELIUS
(impatiently)
No sir, I haven't forgotten.

ZAIUS
Well? For a time the ancients kept humans as household pets. Until the Lawgiver
proved that man could not be tamed. Keep digging Cornelius. You'll find evidence of the
master of this house: an ape.

ANOTHER ANGLE - TO INCLUDE TAYLOR AND NOVA
As Zira again appeals to the man.

ZIRA
Are you going to let that pass without an answer?
Taylor, who has been toying with objects in the dirt, looks up.

TAYLOR
Yes. I have to agree. From all you've found so far, his position's as good as yours.

CORNELIUS
(annoyed)
What are you doing there?

TAYLOR
Reconstructing a life. Care to have a look?
Cornelius and Zira cross the pit and Zaius walks around the rim of the excavation.

B-MED. CLOSE SHOT - FAVORING TAYLOR AND NOVA
As the apes come close. A number of artifacts have been arranged in front of Taylor.

TAYLOR

(to Cornelius)
These were found near the human doll, right?
(Cornelius nods)
Well, whoever owned them was in pretty bad shape.
He picks up the twisted fragment of a pair of spectacles.

TAYLOR
Defective eyesight. .
As Taylor continues his monologue, he picks up the other objects one by one.

TAYLOR
He wore false teeth.
(pause)
He suffered from a hernia and used this truss to hold up his insides ...
(pause)
And toward the end, these little rings of stainless steel enclosed a prefab- ricated valve in his failing heart.
Taylor pauses. Zaius picks up two of the steel rings, studies them.

TAYLOR
I don't say he was a man like an Earthman, but I'd call him a close relative, for he was plagued by most of man's ills.
(to Zaius pointedly)
Yet, fragile as he was, he came before you
-- and was superior to you.

ZAIUS
(a calm smile)
That's lunacy. I can give an alternate description for everyone of those objects that's equally as inventive as yours. But it would be conjecture, not proof.

WIDER ANGLE - TO INCLUDE TAYLOR AND NOVA
She is poking her finger inside the decapitated head of the doll. From it comes a distorted SOUND.

DOLL'S HEAD
Mamma! Mamma! Mamma!.
The apes stare at the doll in astonishment. Taylor snatches the doll from Nova, brandishes it at the astonished Zaius.

TAYLOR
Dr. Zaius! Would an ape make a human doll that talks?

Zaius looks at him, speechless. At that moment the CRACK of a distant rifle shot reverberates through the cavern. All present freeze, listening.

ZIRA
Lucius... .

-
OUT
FULL SHOT - THE CAVERN - REVERSE ANGLE
Taylor alone is armed. Raising his rifle, he glowers at Zaius.

TAYLOR
You louse!
Cornelius is already crossing the pit. He climbs out arid races toward the mouth of the cave. Taylor runs after him. Zira and Nova hurry after
Taylor.

MED. SHOT - ZAIUS
Expressionless, he looks down at the doll, then moves toward the mouth of the cave.

EXT. TRAIL FROM CAVE TO CAMP - ANGLING UP
Cornelius emerges from mouth of the cave and runs down the trail toward
CAMERA. He halts in f. g. , looking down at:

THE CAMP SITE - AS SEEN FROM THE TRAIL
Two of Zaius' gorillas have disarmed Lucius and are clubbing him with their rifle butts. Two other mounted apes are driving the scientists' horses back beyond the trees.

EXT. THE TRAIL - AS SEEN FROM THE BEACH
Cornelius, Taylor, Nova and Zira (in that order) can be seen high above, descending the trail. CAMERA PULLS BACK TO DISCLOSE A GORILLA
SNIPER in immediate f. g. , crouching behind a boulder near the water. He sights his rifle at the man on the trail. Taylor is still too distant to make a sure target, and so the sniper waits.

CLOSER ANGLE - TAYLOR ON THE TRAIL
This portion of the trail has no cover or concealment. Unaware of the sniper, Taylor looks down at the camp as he makes his descent.

LONG SHOT - TAYLOR - AS SEEN IN THE SNIPER'S SIGHTS
The gorilla fires.

CLOSE SHOT - TAYLOR

The bullet ricochets off the rock wall a foot above his head. Taylor scans the terrain bewlow, looking for the sniper. Nova comes to his side, pointing at:

THE SNIPER - FROM THEIR P. O. V.
His head is visible behind the boulder as he reloads his piece.

FLASH SHOT
He aims and fires.

FLASH SHOT - THE SNIPER
Taylor has missed him, but the sniper ducks behind the boulder.

THE TRAIL - PANNING WITH TAYLOR AND NOVA
Taylor takes her hand and they race back up the trail to where Zira is   standing. Outcroppings of rock offer some cover here. Taylor pushes
Nova down behind a rock and signals for Zira to follow suit.

CLOSE GROUP SHOT - TAYLOR, NOVA AND ZIRA
The sniper's SECOND SHOT rings out. Instead of returning the fire,
Taylor looks up the rail at:

ZAIUS - FRO TAYLOR'S P. O. V.
He is standing impassively on the trail a short distance below the mouth of the cave.

FLASH SHOT - TAYLOR
Bent low, he comes charging up the trail toward Zaius. The sniper's
THIRD SHOT splatters rock fragments around him.

REVERSE ANGLE - THE TRAIL - ANGLING UP
Zaius starts to retreat to the cave, but stumbles and falls on some loose shale. No sooner has Zaius regained his feet than Taylor overtakes him. Seizing the ape around the neck with his left arm.
Taylor drives the muzzle of his pistol into Zaius' kidney. He spins
Zaius around, using him as a shield.

CLOSE TWO SHOT - ZAIUS AND TAYLOR
Taylor releases the pressure on Zaius' throat but keeps the gun pointed at his back.

TAYLOR
Tell him to pull back!

ZAIUS
(a hoarse cry)

Cease fire! Withdraw!
His command echoes from the west wall of the canyon.

LONG SHOT - THE FLOOR OF THE GORGE - FROM THEIR P. O. V.
The sniper emerges from behind a boulder near the shore, and walks off along the beach.

BACK TO TAYLOR AND ZAIUS
Taylor lift's the muzzle of his rifle and presses it against the back of Zaius' head.

TAYLOR
I ought to kill you right now.
(nudging him)
Let's go.
They move off down the trail.

EXT. ARCHEOLOGICAL CAMP - MED. SHOT - DAY
Zira rushes down the trail to Lucius, who is sprawled on the ground. He has a bloody
nose and a lump on his forehead. Nova and Cornelius come next, then Taylor, prodding
Zaius ahead of him at gun point. Lucius appears to be more humiliated than hurt.

LUCIUS
They took me by surprise. Sneaked up on me while I was watering the horses. What's
happened to honor?
(pause, glum)
I got off one round to warn you.

CORNELIUS
(gloomingly)
They've taken everything.

TAYLOR
Not everything. They left a hostage.
(a pause)
How do you feel, Lucius?

LUCIUS
Disillusioned...
(turning on)
But vindicated! I've been right all along. You can't trust the older generation. It's a
matter of values --

TAYLOR
(gently)

All right, all right. Will You do me a favor? No orders.

LUCIUS
(pause)
What is it?

TAYLOR
I want you to go around the bend and tell those gorillas their leader is my prisoner.

LUCIUS
(thoughtfull pause)
Yes, I can do that.

TAYLR
Good. Say I want a week's supply of food for the woman and myself. A horse. A spade.
And fifty rounds of ammunition.

LUCIUS
What if they won't agree to your terms?

TAYLOR
Then tell them Dr. Zaius won't leave here alive.

ZIRA
(shocked)
Taylor, you can't.

ZAIUS
(Calmly)
Oh yes he can. He's a born killer.
(to Lucius)
Deliver the message.
Lucius looks to Taylor for confirmation. Taylor nods. The young ape hurries away through the rocks. Taylor crosses to a useless saddle, picks up a coil of rope, gestures at Zaius, indicating a nearby tree.

TAYLOR
Sit down. Over there.
Zaius squats on the ground beside the tree. Taylor sets his rifle against the trunk, fashions a noose and places it around Zaius' neck.
Then, using an ingenious combination of knots, he ties Zaius' hands behind his back, and finally fastens the rope around the base of the tree.

TAYLOR
(as he works)
Now, Minister of Science - let me explain certain principle stress and strain. If you exert pressure to remove these bonds, you'll choke yourself to death. It'll be suicide, you see? Zira and Cornelius look down at the captive mandarin. Their rebellious spirit has evaporated, and they are clearly afraid.

ZIRA
Taylor, please -- don't treat him that way.

TAYLOR
Why not?

ZIRA
It's humiliating.

TAYLOR
Wasn't I humiliated? By all of you?
Didn't you lead me around on a leash?

CORNELIUS
That was different. We thought you were ... . inferior.

TAYLOR
(wintry smile)
And now you know the truth.
(to Zaius)
Cornelius has beaten you, Doctor. He proved it. Man preceded you here. You owe him your science, your language, whatever knowledge you have.

ZAIUS
(quietly)
Then answer this: If ran was superior, why didn't he survive?

TAYLOR
(shrugging)
He might have been wiped out by a plague.
Natural catastrophe. Like a fiery storm of meteors. From the looks of this part of your planet, I'd say that was a fair bet.

ZIRA,
(weakly)
But we can't be sure.

TAYLOR
(indicating Zaius)
He is. He knew all the time. Long before your discovery, he knew.
(to Zaius)
Defender of the Faith. Guardian of the terrible secret. Isn't that right, doctor?

-

OUT
REVERSE ANGLE -CIRCLE - FAVORING ZAIUS
As Zira and Cornelius look at him expectantly.

ZAIUS
What I know of man was written long ago
-- set down by the wisest ape of all -- our Lawgiver.
(to Cornelius)
Open my breast pocket.
Cornelius crosses to Zaius, and takes a small book bound in black leather from the breast pocket of his tunic.

ZAIUS
Read it to him: the twentythird Scroll, ninth Verse.
Cornelius thumbs through the book, finds the citation and reads aloud:

CORNELIUS
'Beware the beast man, for he is the devil's pawn. Alone among God's primates, he kills for sport, or lust or greed.
Yes, he will murder his brother to possess his brother's land. Let him not breed in great numbers, for he will make a desert of his home and yours. Shun him. Drive him back into his jungle lair: For he is the harbinger of death'.
Cornelius falls silent and looks down at Zaius.

ZAIUS
(quietly)
I found nothing in the cave to alter that conception of man. And I still live by its injunction.

ANOTHER ANGLE - THE GROUP
Lucius hurries out of the rocks leading a saddled horse. Zaius' five mounted gorillas appear behind him. Taylor calls out to them:

TAYLOR
Stay where you are!

Lucius comes up with the horse. Taylor checks the provisions in the saddlebags. Lucius is frowning.

LUCIUS
They think you're behaving foolishly. I must say I agree. Where will you go?

TAYLOR
(nodding o. s.)
I'll start by following the shoreline.
(a smile)
And my nose.

ZIRA
But suppose you find nothing but a wasteland. How will you survive?

ZAIUS
(firmly)
He won't survive.
(all look at him)
Do you know what sort of life awaits you out there, Taylor? That of an animal.
If you aren't eventually hunted down and killed by apes, some jungle beast will devour you.

TAYLOR
Then there is another jungle?

ZAIUS
(shrugs; then, sardonically)
Of course, you could return with us. Our society might find a place for you and your mate.

TAYLOR
Sure. In a cage.

ZAIUS
Where else, but in a cage, does man belong?

TAYLOR
No, thanks. I'll take freedom.
Taylor mounts the horse, extends a helping hand to Nova, who vault's nimbly onto the horse's rump. Taylor looks at Zira and Cornelius.

TAYLOR

Would you like to come along?

ZIRA
We can't.

TAYLOR
It's better than going to prison for heresy.

CORNELIUS
They can't convict us of that. You proved our innocence. Besides...
(indicating Zaius)
... his culture is our culture.

TAYLOR
Good luck then.
He reaches down, grasps Cornelius' hand, then grins crookedly.

TAYLOR
Dr. Zira, I'd like to kiss you good-bye.

ZIRA
All right, but... .
(tears in her eyes)
... you're so damned ugly!
Taylor smiles, leans down, kisses her.

ZIRA
(softly)
Go with God, Taylor.
(half smile)
That's an old expression. it comes from both ape and man.

TAYLOR
God bless you.
He extends his hand to Lucius, who takes it.

TAYLOR
Lucius.

LUCIUS
I think you're making a mistake.

TAYLOR

That's the boy. Keep 'em flying.

LUCIUS
What?

TAYLOR
The flags of discontent. It's the only way anything ever gets changed.
(to Zaius)
Don't try to follow us.
(pats stock of his rifle)
I'm pretty handy with things like this.

ZAIUS
Of that I'm sure. All my life I've awaited your coming and dreaded it.
Like death itself.
Taylor looks piercingly at Zaius, more troubled than offended.

TAYLOR
Why? From the first, I've terrified you,
Doctor. And in spite of every sign that
I'm an intelligent being who means no harm, you continue to hate and fear me.
Why?

ZAIUS
(calmly, without rancor)
Because you are a man. And you were right
-- I have always known about man. From the evidence, I believe his wisdom must walk hand in hand with his idiocy. His emotions must rule his brain. He must be a warlike animal who gives battle to everything around him -- even himself.

TAYLOR
What evidence? No weapons were found in the cave.

ZAIUS
The Forbidden Zone was once a paradise.
Your breed made a desert of it, ages ago.

TAYLOR
(he waits, then wearily)
We're back at the beginning. I still don't know the why. A planet where apes evolved from men. A world turned wrong side up.
A puzzle with one piece missing.

ZAIUS
(softly)
Don't look for it, Taylor. You may not like what you find.

B-WIDER ANGLE - TAYLOR AND THE GROUP
Taylor shakes his head, still baffled, digs his heels into the horse's flank. It canters off
along the sandy shore. Zira, Cornelius and
Lucius sadly watch the departure.

ZAIUS
Untie me!
Cornelius moves quickly to remove the rope from Zaius' neck. Behind them, the five
mounted gorillas gallop forward. Zaius gets up, waves them to a halt.

ZAIUS
No, no! Let him go!

C-MOVING SHOT - TAYLOR AND NOVA ON HORSEBACK
Taylor looks back, sees that Zaius has stopped the mounted apes, slows his horse to a
trot, smiles at Nova.

-OUT
MED. SHOT - THE APES
Zaius watches as Taylor's horse moves farther away along the beach.
Then he turns to an ape called MARCUS.

ZAIUS
(quietly)
Fetch your explosives. We're going to seal the cave.

MARCUS
Yes, sir.
He remounts his horse and rides o. s.

CORNELIUS
(aghast)
Seal the cave?

ZAIUS
That's correct. And you will both stand trial for heresy.

ZIRA
But the proof? The doll?

ZAIUS

In a few minutes there will be no doll.
There can't be.
(honest regret)
I'm sorry.
Cornelius throws himself at Zaius.

CORNELIUS

You mustn't! You gave your 'word!
Zaius looks emptily at one of his apes.

ZAIUS

What I do, I do with no pleasure. Silence him.
A hairy hand is clapped over Cornelius' mouth. He is dragged off, struggling, kicking.
Julius, unafraid, glares at Zaius.

LUCIUS

Dr. Zaius, this is inexcusable! Why must knowledge stand still? What about the future?
Zaius looks benevolently at Julius.

ZAIUS

I may just have saved it for you.
Julius and Zira look at each other, befuddled. Once more their eyes follow the retreating
figures of Taylor and Nova. The beach separating the water from the canyon becomes
narrower as they move downstream.

LUCIUS

What will he find out there, doctor?

CLOSEUP - ZAIUS

His face is A mask, his tone enigmatic.

ZAIUS

His destiny.

B-WIDER ANGLE - TIE APES P. O. V.

A moment later, as they watch, Taylor and Nova vanish around the bend.

-OUT

EXT. PALISADE AND BEACH - LONG HIGH ANGLE SHOT - DAY

Taylor and Nova are already far downstream. There is a striking change in the terrain.
The area is still desolate,but some vegetation can be

seen on the palisade above the narrow beach, and the river has widened to form a vast tidal basin where it meets the sea.
A NOTE ON PRODUCTION: If feasible at new location site, this scene should be shot at high tide, so that the water laps at the base of the cliffs, making a passage difficult and risky.

CLOSER ANGLE - PANNING WITH TAYLOR AND NOVA ON HORSEBACK
He is alert, sniffing the salt air, sizing up the situation. Hearing the CRIES of birds, he reins in and looks' up.

SKY SHOT - CIRCLING BIRDS
Sea gulls are soaring overhead.

TWO SHOT - TAYLOR AND NOVA ON HORSEBACK
His expression is expectant, searching. Nova emits a whimper of anticipation, pointing off.

LONG SHOT - WHAT THEY SEE:
A verdant forest atop a distant palisade. Their view of the beach below the forest, is cut off by a rocky promontory in the middle distance.

CLOSE SHOT - NOVA AND TAYLOR
He smiles at her hopefully.

TAYLOR
Yes, Nova -- I see it.
(looks again at forest)
In my old profession green meant safe. Green meant go.
The horse moves off at a trot, CAMERA PANNING. But they have gone only a short distance when they hear the distant THUNDER of an EXPLOSION.
Taylor reins in and looks back.

VERY LONG SHOT - A CLOUD OF SMOKE
A column of smoke and dust rises from the exploded cave far upstream.

BACK TO TAYLOR AND NOVA
Frowning with concern, Taylor gazes for a moment at the smoke, then decides this is no time to linger. He digs his heels into the horse's flanks and they move off at a canter, riding toward the promontory that splits the beach. They are nearing the promontory that blocks their view of the beach beyond.

-OUT
CLOSER ANGLE - TRACKING WITH TAYLOR AND NOVA.

As they round the promontory, the tip of a strange rock formation comes into view. it appears to be jutting from the sea.

REACTION SHOT - TAYLOR
He reins in momentarily, baffled by what he sees. Then he rides on.

THE STRANGE FORMATION - AS SEEN BY TAYLOR
An immense column juts from the beach at a thirty-degree angle. We can now see that it is not rock, but metal. Green metallic tints show through its gray salt-stained surface. As we draw closer, the object takes on the appearance of a massive arm, its top shaped like a hand holding a torch.

REVERSE ANGLE - FAVORING TAYLOR
Frowning with consternation. His horse proceeds at a slow walk.

TRACKING WITH TAYLOR - WHAT HE SEES:
Near the base of the column, where the shore and water meet, are a row of metal spikes. From this angle they look like tank traps.

CLOSER - TAYLOR
Dumbfounded, he slides from his saddle, approaches the spikes. Nova dismounts and follows him.

TAYLOR
(a cry of agony)
My God!
He falls to his knees, buries his head in his hands. CAMERA SLOWLY
DRAWS BACK AND UP to a HIGH ANGLE SHOT disclosing what Taylor has found.
Half-buried in the sand and washed by the waves is the Statue of
Liberty.

FADE OUT
THE END